ppeasement

5 111 824 6

General Editors: *Muriel Chamberlain, H. T. Dickinson and Joe Smith*

Titles in Print

China in the Twentieth Century
Paul Bailey
Postwar Japan: 1945 to the Present
Paul Bailey
The Agricultural Revolution
John Beckett
Class, Party and the Political System in
Britain 1867–1914
John Belchem
Ireland 1828–1923: From Ascendancy to
Democracy
D. George Boyce
The British Welfare State: A Critical
History
John Brown
Decolonization: The Fall of the
European Empires
M. E. Chamberlain
From Luddism to the First Reform Bill:
Reform in England 1810–1832
J. R. Dinwiddy
Radicalism in the English Revolution
1640–1660
F. D. Dow
British Politics Since 1945: The Rise
and Fall of Consensus
David Dutton
The Spanish Civil War
Sheelagh M. Ellwood
The French Revolution
Alan Forrest
Oliver Cromwell
Peter Gaunt
The French Reformation
Mark Greengrass
Occupied France: Collaboration and
Resistance 1940–1944
H. R. Kedward
The Vikings in Britain
Henry Loyn
Women in an Industrializing Society:
England 1750–1880
Jane Rendall

Appeasement (Second Edition)
Keith Robbins
Britain's Decline: Problems and
Perspectives
Alan Sked
Britain in the 1930s
Andrew Thorpe
The Normans in Britain
David Walker
Bismarck
Bruce Waller
The Russian Revolution 1917–1921
Beryl Williams
The Making of Modern South Africa
(Second Edition)
Nigel Worden
Lloyd George
Chris Wrigley

Forthcoming titles

Germany under the Nazis
Richard Bessel
British Politics 1832–1885
John Bourne
The Italian Renaissance
Peter Denley
The Whig Supremacy
H. T. Dickinson
The German Reformation
C. Scott Dixon
The Enlightenment
Martin Fitzpatrick
The American Revolution
Keith Mason
Gladstone
Neville Masterman
The Cold War (Second Edition)
Joe Smith
John F. Kennedy
Geoff Stoakes

The Historical Association, founded in 1906, brings together people who share an interest in, and love for, the past. It aims to further the study and teaching of history at all levels: teacher and student, amateur and professional. This is one of over 100 publications available at preferential rates to members. Membership also includes journals at generous discounts and gives access to courses, conferences, tours and regional and local activities. Full details are available from The Secretary, The Historical Association, 59a Kennington Park Road, London SE11 4JH, telephone: 0171-735 3901.

Appeasement
Second Edition

Keith Robbins

The right of Keith Robbins to be identified as author of this work has been asserted in accordance with the Copyright, Designs and Patents Act 1988.

First published 1988
Reprinted 1991
Second edition published 1997

First published in USA 1997
2 4 6 8 10 9 7 5 3 1

Blackwell Publishers Ltd
108 Cowley Road
Oxford OX4 1JF
UK

Blackwell Publishers, Inc.
Commerce Place
350 Main Street
Malden, MA 02148
USA

British Library Cataloguing in Publication Data
A CIP catalogue record for this book is available from the British Library.

Library of Congress Cataloging-in-Publication Data

Robbins, Keith.
    Appeasement / Keith Robbins. — 2nd ed.
    101p. — (Historical Association studies)
    Includes bibliographical references and index.
    ISBN 0-631-20326-5 (alk. paper)
    1. Great Britain—Foreign relations—Germany. 2. Great Britain—
Foreign relations—1936-1945. 3. Germany—Foreign relations—Great Britain.
4. Germany—Foreign relations—1933-1945. 5. World War, 1939-1945—Causes.
I. Title. II. Series.
DA47.2.R62   1997
327.41043—dc21   96-44376
                                                                                     CIP

Typeset in 11 on 13 pt Ehrhardt by Ace Filmsetting Ltd, Frome, Somerset
Printed in Great Britain by Hartnolls Limited, Bodmin, Cornwall

This book is printed on acid-free paper

Contents

1

Historiography

'Appeasement' has had a bad press for a long time. Fifty years after its *annus mirabilis* in 1938, it is time to take stock. There is no lack of literature on the subject. Conceived and executed in dramatic circumstances, it has continued to engage the passionate attention of politicians and historians ever since. Scarcely a year has gone by without a substantial contribution to the debate appearing, but, predictably and for historians fortunately, there is no sign of consensus. Yet the nature of the discussion has changed considerably, and indeed it would be strange if it had not done so. The 1930s now seem very far away and it is difficult to recapture the assumptions of those who tried to steer the foreign policy of what then appeared to be the greatest empire in the world. The historiography of the subject is inevitably influenced by the substantial shifts that have since taken place in global politics.

Appeasement was not a 'success' for long enough to allow contemporaries to praise its merits in any depth. In 1938 itself, the year of Munich, there were some historians who believed that government policy was broadly on the right lines. The balance of newspaper comment was also in agreement. Measured reflection on the merits of the policy was not made easy by the outbreak of war in September 1939. Churchill, who became Prime Minister in the following spring, distanced himself at every opportunity from those who held power in the preceding decade. It was tempting to believe that appeasement had produced the catastrophe from which he was in process of rescuing the country. Churchill encouraged that belief. The Second World War was not the time for historians to embark on a defence of British foreign policy in the heyday of 'appeasement'. At its conclusion, Churchill's description of the conflict as 'the unnecessary war' gained authority from the fact that, fortunately, he had seen to it that things had turned out right in the end.

Or had they? 'Success' and 'failure' frequently lie in the eye of the beholder. In his more gloomy post-war moments, even Churchill privately felt that he had failed. He told his cousin that his life and work had all been for nothing: 'The Empire I believed in has gone' (Callahan, 1984, p. 265). Coming to terms with 'appeasement' involves nothing less than grappling with the fate of Britain in twentieth-century world politics. Churchill could rightly claim that his ebullient leadership had helped Britain escape the fate of becoming a mere *Gau* or province in a Nazi-dominated Europe; but it is not to belittle the efforts of the British people to point out that the Prime Minister had more than his fair share of luck. It is also apparent that Britain could never have won the war on its own. There was, in consequence, a price to be paid for collaborative victory. Churchill himself was well aware of the fact that, by the end of the war, Britain was the smallest of the Big Three, somewhat dwarfed by the United States and the Soviet Union. He had publicly proclaimed his determination not to preside over the liquidation of the British Empire. Instead, he bequeathed the commencement of this operation to Attlee and the post-war Labour administrations. We now know that Labour set about this task with less than whole-hearted enthusiasm. Churchill had set great store upon his own 'special relationship' with President Roosevelt, but whatever might be the quality of that relationship, events after 1945 disclosed that the Anglo-American partnership was not one between equals. The United States set the agenda of the alliance, and while successive British foreign secretaries might have 'influence', the mould was cast. A position of some privilege in a rather uncertain *Pax Americana* was not, perhaps, ideal, but there were worse alternatives.

After 1945, too, Britain still had to work out a relationship with 'Europe'. Churchill collected honorary degrees and talked archly about a United States of Europe, though Britain would not be included. The Labour government would have no truck with federalism, but its Foreign Secretary Ernest Bevin was prepared to work towards some measure of closer co-operation. It has been supposed that during this crucial period Britain missed the European bus: Bevin did not think there was a scheduled service going in the direction Britain's interests required. Finally, after 1945, there was the new reality of the Soviet Union ensconced in large areas of Eastern Europe, a power of at least potentially menacing character.

That was the kind of world in which the first 'historical' attempts to write about 'appeasement' took place. British historians wrote about the pre-war years with a mixture of satisfaction and revulsion. Victory was too obvious a fact to be able to question its implications. The cloak of Churchill enveloped early accounts. It did not take the poet W. H. Auden to discover that the 1930s had been a 'low dishonest decade'. The historian Lewis Namier, an expert reviewer, smelt incipient 'collaborators' as he ruthlessly dissected the recollections and memoirs of such politicians and diplomats as dared to publish. The then fifty-year rule governing access to official papers prevented access to the British documents of the period, but in 1944 it had been agreed that volumes of selected documents covering the entire inter-war period would appear. Such was the obvious interest in the years immediately leading up to the outbreak of war in Europe that they were among the first to be published, roughly a decade after the events to which they referred. They were quarried by all serious writers on the topic, but what is significant is that they appeared in isolation. It took decades for the series of volumes which had 1929 as its starting year to reach the mid-1930s. Indeed, the volume on European affairs from July 1937 to August 1938 did not appear until 1982. In the 1950s and 1960s, therefore, a certain frozen perspective was evident. Books still focused on the 'high summer' of appeasement, but their authors had little or no documentary knowledge of the problems and issues which had preoccupied previous administrations and which formed an essential preliminary to understanding the events of 1938–9. A particular consequence of this publication policy was that it perpetuated an approach to appeasement which was thoroughly Eurocentric. It was easy to draw the conclusion from the volumes published in 1949 on the years 1938–9 that the British Empire did not exist, since it did not feature in them. It could appear that ministers evidently had nothing better to do than worry about 'Europe'. Historians followed suit. And, as the Cold War became colder in the Europe of their day – and Czechoslovakia again suffered a melancholy fate – such an emphasis seemed quite appropriate.

By the time another decade had elapsed, however, it was becoming evident, even to traditional historians of British diplomacy, that the world beyond Europe did occasionally impinge. The *raj* had been surrendered and the mandate in Palestine had become too uncomfortable to be maintained. However we explain it, 'decolonization' seemed to be gathering pace. Then came the Suez crisis of 1956. This episode had at least two aspects which are relevant to our theme. In the first place, it showed that if a British government wished to follow a policy disapproved of by the government of the United States it did so at its peril. It was publicly and humiliatingly demonstrated that the relationship between Washington and London was not one between equals. The British Empire/Commonwealth had not survived the war unscathed. Maybe Britain was still a Great Power, but it was in eclipse. In the second place, Suez had occasioned an elaborate display of 'anti-appeasement' rhetoric which had an appeal across the British party divide. It was argued that President Nasser of Egypt was an ambitious, unstable, aggressive dictator. Unless stopped, he would, 'like Hitler', have even more ambitious ideas. British politicians claimed to be applying the 'lessons' of the 1930s and tried to label their opponents 'appeasers'. However, President Nasser survived. 'Appeasement' might still have been 'bad' in the 1930s, but there were evidently circumstances in which its alternative might not be feasible.

Against this background, a new generation of British historians began to wonder whether the world of the 1960s, in which they were attaining their academic maturity, had fresh questions to ask of those who had made policy in the 1930s. The Second World War, which this generation only experienced as infants, did not seem to have settled as much as their parents and teachers appeared to believe. British governments wrestled with the problems of the Commonwealth, of Europe, of the Soviet Union and of the United States without conspicuous success. These were the years when Dean Acheson, a well-disposed United States Secretary of State, made his remark that Britain had lost an Empire and had not yet found a new role. Such a condition could surely not have come about overnight. Maybe the 1930s was a crucial decade in a sense never hitherto understood. It stood approximately at the half-way point between the signing of agreements with Japan, France and Russia in the years from 1902 to 1907, and a dissolving Empire and fumblings towards 'Europe' in the late 1960s. It might be possible at least to understand appeasement better if it were seen as a central episode in a protracted retreat from an untenable 'world power' status. Appeasement, on such an analysis, was neither stupid nor wicked: it was merely inevitable.

Since no historian writes in a vacuum, it may be helpful to reveal the circumstances in which I first came to consider the question of appeasement. Having read the available historical literature, I was quite convinced, as an undergraduate, that the policy had been morally wrong and politically disastrous. However, I was taught by A.J.P. Taylor, who published his *The Origins of the Second World War* (1961) in the year I graduated. A few years later, I was invited to write a book on the Munich crisis which was to appear in print thirty years after the crisis ended. I was attracted to the topic partly because I had not even been alive during the appeasement years and wanted to approach the entire topic afresh without the emotions which still so clearly troubled an older generation. In retrospect, however, the early 1960s appears as a twilight period. Old preconceptions were still vigorous, though the speed with which Martin Gilbert, later well known as the biographer of Churchill, altered his emphasis in *The Roots of Appeasement* (1966) from that adopted a few years earlier in *The Appeasers*, which he wrote with Richard Gott, indicates a changing climate. Even so, it was *Munich*

1938 that the publishers supposed that my readers would want, as the anniversary drew near, not a general exposition of appeasement. My approach was therefore, in a sense, 'traditional', though there was within it a disinclination to separate sheep from goats in writing about the 'appeasers'. Reading it again, twenty years later, it seems a transitional book. It appears to say farewell to the preoccupations and prejudices of the years since 1945 but leaves open the future direction of research and criticism.

On the eve of the publication of *Munich 1938* in 1968 the fifty-year rule postponing access to official papers was changed to a thirty-year rule. Immediately, many scholars immersed themselves in the mass of documentation that became available. Additional private papers also became accessible. The result was a flood of monographs and articles. It is only recently that the volume of publication has slowed down somewhat as post-1945 international history has become the centre of attention. This research became truly international, with notable contributions to the study of 'appeasement' being made by British, American and German scholars. While it is impossible to speak of historians conforming to 'national' schools in this matter, there are differences in style and technique which follow something of a national pattern.

The outcome, however, is that it has become more difficult to speak about 'appeasement' in simple terms. Rather, we are apparently confronted by a series of policies which can be described as forms of appeasement or which together make up appeasement. There is 'economic appeasement', 'military appeasement', 'political appeasement' and 'social appeasement'. Needless to say, it is not easy to determine how one aspect relates to another and which is 'primary' and which 'secondary'. It is tempting, in such circumstances, to follow the advice of the late Professor Medlicott and argue that appeasement is not a term any historian should use, since its meaning has become so general. That advice is wise but, since it stands no chance of being observed in the world at large, it will be ignored. The opposite temptation – to embark on an elaborate and exhaustive definition 'excluding all other' – will also be avoided. It is common to speak of appeasement as a policy, but it will become evident that men who thought of themselves as appeasers could advocate different specific policies. It is perhaps better conceived as an underlying attitude of mind deriving variously, in particular instances, from fear, guilt, superiority, insecurity or hope of economic advantage. It can be summarized as a disposition to anticipate and avoid conflict by judicious concession and negotiation. There can be no agreement, however, on what is 'judicious'. A particular adjustment may seem 'reasonable' but appear in an 'unreasonable' sequence. Appeasement may appear to be a particularly British phenomenon of the twentieth century; a fusion of moral values, political constraints, economic necessities and military exigencies. In a general sense, there is scarcely a British government in recent decades which has not been willing to appear conciliatory in its general stance. Nevertheless, it remains sensible to think of appeasement as a phenomenon of the 1930s and to describe as 'appeasers' those who were then responsible for both the formulation and the execution of policy. Even if what was being attempted was, in a longer perspective, an elaboration of earlier insights and attitudes, its articulation was novel. After the 1930s, appeasement did not disappear from British foreign policy; it was simply called something different .

In addition, in the 1990s, attitudes towards appeasement have in part been affected by the reconsideration of the significance, for Britain, of the Second World War itself. The public celebrations in Britain of the fiftieth anniversary of its conclusion could not altogether disguise the ambiguous character of 'victory'. The fact that, for a time, the British people had stood alone against Hitler was no doubt to their enduring credit, but the cost had been high, perhaps too high. Some historians delighted in exposing the flaws in Churchill's character and puncturing the patriotic myths which still surrounded the British view of the Second World War. The strategy pursued by the great opponent of appeasement, it was suggested, led to a bankrupt Britain, the collapse of the British Empire, Soviet ascendancy in Eastern Europe and Britain itself as little more than an American dependency. Britain/the British Empire was not the Great Power Churchill had initially supposed it still to be. In December 1944, for example, there was a widespread feeling in the Foreign Office that Churchill was erroneously pursuing a 'policy of appeasement' towards Moscow and Washington. *The Economist* publicly demanded that an end should be put to such a policy. (Reynolds in Dockrill and McKercher, 1996, p. 198). Here was the sad end of British glory (Charmley, 1993). It was almost a matter of luck that, in what turned out to be a global conflict, Britain emerged on the winning side. Such ideas were in turn vigorously contested in whole or in part. There was great scepticism about the enduring feasibility, let alone the propriety, of any conceivable alternative 'division of spheres' with Hitler. Even so, it has led some historians to praise Chamberlain for the lengths to which he was prepared to go to avoid the 'victorious catastrophe' which eventually followed his failure.

The chapters that follow will look at particular aspects of appeasement in Britain, but there is a danger in seeing it as something 'the British' invented and controlled. Foreign policy is about the complex and constantly changing relations of states. The games are intricate and the rules suspect. Appeasement was both a domestically generated initiative and an externally generated response. A British government might have been in a position, up to a point, to determine how Britain should behave, but it could not control the lobs dropped into its court by Hitler, Mussolini, Gandhi or Roosevelt, to mention but four names.

It is tempting, sometimes, to believe that appeasement ought to have worked and would have done so but for the disagreeable reaction of foreigners; but a foreign policy which misjudges foreigners' likely responses is apt to fail.

2

Policy and Party Politics

Appeasement, it is generally agreed, stemmed from the particular circumstances of British domestic politics in the years after 1919. At one level, of course, such an observation is a mere truism. British governments were at the mercy of British electorates. 'Public opinion' could not be ignored. Equally, however, it was far from clear how foreign policy should be conducted in a democracy. The British decision to go to war in 1914 illustrated this point sharply. Sir Edward Grey, the Foreign Secretary, had been given considerable latitude by his Cabinet colleagues and had not believed in 'open diplomacy' or substantial public consultation. Britain could not have gone to war if the House of Commons had turned against him in August but, by that stage, rightly or wrongly, intervention was in practical terms difficult to prevent. The swing of opinion in the country at large took place at a very late stage.

The war of 1914–18 led to two important developments. Initial assumptions of a short war and 'business as usual' had fairly rapidly to be abandoned. By propaganda and other means it proved necessary to buttress support for a war that was indeed still fundamentally accepted. 'Total war' now required the mobilization of all the energies and resources of the nation. Such was the nature of mass participation that commentators found it increasingly difficult to conceive of a successful war ever being fought by a state of whose population a substantial proportion was in some way or other disaffected. Secondly, the war played havoc with the British party system. Major changes took place in the fortunes of individual politicians and in the structure of party politics without benefit of a General Election. Its historians can argue endlessly about whether the Liberal Party was destroyed by the exigencies of the war or whether it was already in acute decline. The fact remains that in 1918–19 the Liberal Party was in a grave condition. It appeared that the party structure might change profoundly. In one way or another, it can be argued that the 'challenge of Labour' confronted all the politicians who had come to prominence before 1914 and were to be still in office in 1939. The uncertainty was compounded by the major extension of the franchise, among males in 1918 and partially and then universally among females in 1918 and 1928. The politicians who aspired to office in the 1929 General Election were all appealing to a very different electorate from that which, through its MPs, endorsed the decision to go to war in 1914. The relationship between this new democracy, based on universal suffrage, and foreign policy, might have to be worked out afresh in an international environment which was scarcely stable.

During the war, a group of intellectuals, publicists and Liberal, ex-Liberal and Labour politicians had formed the Union of Democratic Control. In the view of this group, the outbreak of war in 1914 had shown the futility and inappropriateness of existing diplomatic procedures and assumptions. Secret diplomacy belonged to a bygone era. It was time to involve 'the people' in policy-making, or at least to ensure that there was indeed a democratic control over decision-making. There was an assumption that 'the people' were inherently pacific and had only been involved in wars by the machinations of elites who initiated conflicts for their own ends. These views had some influence. They blended with the contempt for secret treaties apparently displayed both by the Bolsheviks and by US President Wilson. They also related, although a little awkwardly, to the enthusiasm for a League of Nations displayed by the centre and left in British politics. However, when it came to details, there was little unanimity about how either 'democratic control' or the League of Nations was to work. For some, 'democratic control' went beyond mere parliamentary control and there was talk of plebiscites and referenda. Others concentrated on trying to devise mechanisms whereby the executive would be subjected to scrutiny and restraint by various foreign policy committees of the House of Commons. The more these matters were considered, the more difficult it became to locate both 'public opinion' and 'foreign policy'. A similar range of views surrounded the League of Nations. Some supporters saw it as an embryonic world government with 'effective' military sanctions at its disposal. Others believed that its essential purpose was to provide a forum for international debate and discussion. Enthusiasts supposed that its creation would render obsolete the notion of a specific British foreign policy.

In any event, supporters either of 'democratic control' or of the League of Nations were not in power during the 1920s. Labour did form a short-lived minority government in January 1924 but was in no position to attempt major changes in either the conduct or content of policy – to the dismay of UDC supporters. Coalition or Conservative governments predominated – though they too could not ignore the changed atmosphere. The League of Nations, at least in theory, enjoyed the support of all political parties. Nevertheless, Conservatives were still certain that there was a British national interest and that British policy could not be completely subordinated to the requirements of the League. Indeed, there was in many Conservative quarters a deep if disguised scepticism about the utility of the League. Its most vocal party champion, Lord Robert Cecil, lacked political weight inside the party. A dangerous gap opened between public professions of support for the League and private estimates of its value. It remained impossible, however, to denounce the new organization since it seemed to many to be the enduring symbol of the fact that the Great War had indeed been the war to end war. Even so, traditional diplomacy still had a part to play – as the policy followed by Conservative Foreign Secretary Sir Austen Chamberlain demonstrated. Yet the Foreign Office, still saddled with responsibility for the supposedly disastrous 'balance of power' policies of the pre-1914 era, had ground to make up to regain the role it had then played. Additionally, Lloyd George had developed his own ways of conducting policy; and though, after his fall, traditional ways did indeed regain ground, they never recovered it completely. There was also a school of thought that believed that improved communications and the possibility of face-to-face encounters between leading politicians made ambassadors largely redundant. It was increasingly supposed, too, that the Foreign Office was too narrowly 'political' at a time when commercial and financial matters were of extreme importance. As the 1930s opened, therefore, circumstances made it far from easy to say precisely how British policy was made or how successfully it could be implemented. Foreign observers were not alone in being unable to distinguish between rhetoric and reality.

There was, however, an underlying national consensus that British participation in another war was, to say the least, undesirable. It would be an overstatement to suggest that most British opinion in the 1920s believed that it had been wrong to take part in the Great War. It was still generally accepted that it would have been wrong to stand aside. Nevertheless, from a British standpoint, the outcome already seemed ambiguous. Considered either from a narrowly political standpoint or from an ethical perspective the gains and losses seemed about equal. It was difficult to believe that there would be circumstances in the future which would justify a struggle of such protracted ferocity. Britain's primary task, therefore, was to seek to reduce the likelihood of general war and to ensure it was not dragged into one if it did occur. Only a drastic change of international circumstances might promote a reassessment of this national assumption.

It was easy, at least in retrospect, to see three main zones within which British policy would have to function if this underlying objective was to be achieved. The first was the European continent. It might be supposed that close collaboration with France in particular would have consolidated the pre-war entente into an enduring alliance. On the contrary, the prevailing mood was to minimize the European connexion. Britain was an off-shore island compelled reluctantly to intervene but unwilling to form permanent alliances. Its role was to act, so far as possible, as an arbiter; a course facilitated by detachment rather than commitment. Britain could not stand entirely aloof, but it was highly desirable that the

European powers should sort out their own problems. There was an emotional as much as a rational reaction in this pervasive attitude. Ambivalence remained, however, since Britain had not helped defeat the German attempt to achieve European hegemony merely to see the French operating as though the continent were theirs to direct. Geography compelled Britain to take a close interest in continental developments; but in a spiritual sense Britain was not a European power.

One reason for this detachment was, of course, the British Empire. In the early 1920s there was a renewed belief in and enthusiasm for its prospects. Britain became responsible for the administration of Palestine, Iraq and Tanganyika under a 'mandate' from the League of Nations. Technically, these countries were not annexed, but it could be said that the British Empire had never before included so many diverse territories. For some it was time at last to exploit what Joseph Chamberlain had earlier referred to as the 'undeveloped estate'. Great encouragement was given to overseas emigration from the United Kingdom. Expectations were to prove exaggerated but at the time they were real. It was difficult to judge the health of the non-selfgoverning British Empire. Naturally, both on the spot and in London, assessments differed. Some pointed to the magnificent response (as they perceived it) of the Empire as a whole to the war effort. Such a contribution demonstrated the vitality of imperial sentiment. Other observers were less impressed and pointed instead to signs of increasing dissatisfaction with the imperial system on the part of subject peoples. Perhaps the most conspicuous example of difficulty was India. Certain changes in its government were made in 1919, but they did not go far enough for some sections of Indian opinion. No doubt dissent could be contained in the short term, but the ultimate future of the *raj* was beginning to look more uncertain. To maintain control simply on the basis of superior force would entail unimaginable military commitments. On the other hand, if India were to become independent, this might well signify the end of empire – at least as it had traditionally been conceived. And India was only one example. British control, formal or informal, over large areas of the Middle East looked very impressive, but discontent in Egypt and elsewhere was already very vocal. At the political level, however, it appeared that the British Empire was adjusting to new circumstances. The formula agreed at the 1926 imperial conference in London recognized the reality of Dominion self-government. These members of the British Empire were not subordinate to each other in status, though other implications had still to be worked out, notably in the sphere of defence. The impulse to collaborate was still strong. There seemed, therefore, good reason to believe that this second area of policy was fundamental if Britain wished to maintain her global standing. What was obscure was the price which would have to be paid in order to do so.

The third zone of policy concerned the United States. The Anglo-American relationship was complex and cannot easily be summarized. There was a recognition that American assistance had been vital in the final stages of the Great War. Without it, Britain and France might have been defeated. On the other hand, there remained a certain irritation that in 1914 the United States had been neutral and that President Wilson had not then been able to distinguish between the merits of the opposing sides. There was also apprehension that the United States would seek to play a world role commensurate with the strength it had latterly displayed. That influence might be exerted in ways contrary to British interests. In fact, of course, the United States did not seek that role, at least not in a political sense, and assumptions had to be revised. Professor Watt has identified four bodies of British opinion in these circumstances: 'nationalists' who bitterly resented the extent to which the United States had intruded into what they regarded as British spheres – the Middle East, for example; Americophiles who saw Britain as an Atlantic power and the United States as populated by fellow-members of the 'English-speaking world'; neo-imperialists who thought the United States might be an obstacle to a rejuvenated Empire; and finally a large but amorphous group of British politicians who thought that the United States was the most appropriate power with which Britain might co-operate – though different British politicians looked to different Americans as their perfect counterparts (Watt, 1985, p. 49). It is not surprising that these often contradictory objectives produced confused policy outcomes. There was agreement, however, that whether as challenger or partner the United States was the coming power in the world. Evidently its moment had not quite arrived and its relative isolation from world affairs appeared to give Britain's world-power status a slightly surprising extended lease of life.

The fundamental task before British policy-makers was to keep their eyes on these three zones and to seek to promote a beneficial interplay between them. The difficulty of the enterprise should not be underestimated. History and geography combined to make the management of British foreign policy the most complex in the world as it then existed. While the machinery of government was sophisticated, the proliferation of British interests and commitments across the world meant that it was difficult to maintain a truly synoptic view. The Foreign Office did its best but the input from the Government of India, the Colonial Office and the new Dominions Office could offer a rather different perspective on world developments. It is not surprising that any upheaval in any part of the world would be against British interests. Peace preserved a congenial status quo.

A decade after the end of the Great War, there existed in government circles a reasonable confidence that immediate post-war problems had been overcome. The new Labour government was in a position to build on what had been achieved by Sir Austen Chamberlain in promoting Franco–German accommodation, apparently successfully. At this juncture, it seemed that the self-interested concern for peace on the part of traditional elites fused neatly with an attitude towards issues of war and peace which was more emotional and intense. Men and women on the left and in the centre of British politics did not 'merely' incline towards peace because it seemed in Britain's interests as an imperial power. Indeed, for many of them, being an imperial power was a source of embarrassment rather than pride. Peace for them was an end in itself, to be advocated as perhaps the supreme good. This attitude of mind can be broadly labelled 'pacifist'. It embraced both the small minority who vowed never to fight again in any cause and the much larger number who might conceivably fight if war should come but who were to devote all their efforts to ensuring that it did not. Looking back at 1914 in particular, a conviction developed that it was possible to explain how and why wars started. Diplomacy based on the 'balance of power' was clearly mistaken since it falsely presupposed that international relations were fundamentally adversarial in nature. In any event, there was no such thing as a 'balance of power' but rather a situation of perpetual instability as states sought to tip the 'balance' in their favour. The idea of 'collective security', based on the premise that all states were fundamentally in favour of peace, and would join together to uphold it, was a much better one. Despite its imperfections, the League of Nations attempted to embody this principle. Secondly, it was argued that the existence of major armed forces constituted a threat to peace since there was always a danger that arms races would develop out of control. In such quarters, therefore, it was deemed neither sufficient nor satisfactory that Germany had been disarmed while France maintained a large army. One-sided disarmament might appear to enhance Britain's security but in reality it fuelled a German sense of grievance. It followed that multilateral disarmament was urgent and a world conference to this end was vital. Thirdly, it was often argued that the treaty of Versailles and the other settlements at the end of the Great War had been misconceived, and that it was a mistake to believe that their provisions could or should be sustained in perpetuity. The treatment of Germany had been too severe; a peace imposed by victors would not endure and it was better to contemplate some revision on a basis more acceptable to the defeated nation.

These three perspectives on war and peace were mostly to be found within the Labour Party, though many Liberals and even some Conservatives shared them. What was specific to Labour, however, was the notion of a 'Socialist foreign policy'. Prior to 1914, many Liberals had wanted their government to follow a specifically Liberal policy – for example, in relation to Russia. However, general diplomatic considerations seemed to require a convention with the Tsarist government and their criticisms were largely ignored. Within the growing Labour Party, however, there was an insistence that 'Socialist principles' should not be subordinated to alleged national requirements. It would be no part of a Labour government's duty to maintain continuity in foreign policy. It would probably be necessary to sweep away the archaic structures of the Foreign Office. It would also be vital to break with established attitudes towards the new Soviet state.

Certainly, the survival of the Soviet Union brought a new element into both international and British domestic politics. At the close of the war, a vigorous campaign against the Bolsheviks had been contemplated by the Coalition government but in the end full-scale intervention was rejected. The Soviet Union was at once a state in a conventional sense and also, at least in theory, the solitary embodiment of the interests of the world proletariat. By definition, it could not refrain from interesting itself in the internal affairs of other countries on behalf of their proletariats. A new and unpredictable element had entered into the international system. The Labour Party, as it emerged from the war, was not a Bolshevik party, nevertheless, it did not favour any action designed to overthrow Bolshevism. When it came into government, Labour granted the Soviet Union *de jure* recognition and thus made possible diplomatic relations with Moscow in a gesture of a mildly ideological character. Within a few years, in May 1927, succeeding Conservative government broke off relations in protest at Soviet activity in London. This step pointed to the highly-charged relationship between domestic politics and foreign policy. The letter, allegedly sent by Zinoviev from the Third International's headquarters in Moscow to the British Communist Party, inciting it to subversion, had played a part in Labour's General Election defeat. A Labour government would no doubt restore diplomatic relations but it would tread warily. The ambiguity of its attitude was in turn a reflection of its own ambiguity towards capitalism. Once again it had no overall parliamentary majority and could not 'abolish' British capitalism. It was not even sure that it wanted to do so. Similarly, it was always easier to frame a Socialist foreign policy in opposition than to implement it in government.

As the 1930s opened, therefore, Britain still appeared in many respects to be a highly consensual society. Within the preceding decade, a Labour Party had emerged from impotence into government (though it still lacked the authority conferred by an overall parliamentary majority). Of course, many of its opponents were apprehensive about the future. Perhaps universal suffrage meant perpetual Labour government. Nevertheless, there was little inclination among Conservatives – in contrast to what was beginning to happen on the European mainland – to seek merely to defend certain vested interests or to flirt with a radical Right. The Conservative party, given the context of disintegrating Liberalism, would seek to remain a national party with a cross-class appeal. The 1926 general strike had shown the extent of division within the country but, in general, Baldwin at least did not appear apprehensive about his party's prospects. Much depended upon the social policies a future Conservative government might follow. The ability of the British apparently to accomplish political change within an old parliamentary framework during these years has been taken to have wider significance. In a sense, here was the 'politics of appeasement' at work in a domestic context. Government and opposition disagreed but could co-exist. Civil society did not fall apart in conflict. British politicians of all parties noted that this capacity for compromise, however it might be explained, did not seem much in evidence elsewhere in Europe. Even so, there remained a strong belief that 'give and take' should become universal good practice. There was also an assumption that this domestic mode of behaviour could or should be relevant to the world of states. Differences of perspective and interest were perhaps inevitable in the international arena but they were capable of peaceful resolution, especially in the light of what was already known about the nature of the twentieth-century warfare.

The decade that followed was to witness a succession of question marks, to say the least, placed against the assumptions so far outlined which governed British politics in both its domestic and its international aspects. There had been serious crises in the 1920s – Chanak, the Ruhr, Shanghai – but there was no sense of impending interlocking global conflict. In such circumstances policy differences within and between governments did not seem to involve decisions which could lead to a major war. Within a short period that comfortable state of affairs began to disappear. A sustainable international order suddenly seemed vulnerable to fresh challenges. To an extent, the problems could be compartmentalized – and they will be looked at separately in subsequent chapters – but the crisis showed every sign of becoming general.

In domestic terms, British party politics followed a course which few would have predicted. In 1931 a divided Labour government wrestled unsuccessfully with a financial crisis. Ramsay MacDonald, the Prime Minister, accepted the King's invitation to form a new administration. Few Labour colleagues followed him in this course and the new government depended upon Conservative and Liberal support. In the General Election that followed, the Labour Party suffered massive electoral defeat. It appeared that National government would not be a mere short-term expedient as originally advertised. Indeed, there was to be a National government in office for the remainder of the decade. The administrations were in practice heavily dependent upon the support of Conservative MPs, whose party remained by far the largest in the House of Commons. In 1935 Baldwin became Prime Minister and achieved a considerable majority in the General Election. He made way for Neville Chamberlain in May 1937. A further General Election was in prospect in 1939. Some government ministers were apprehensive about their chances of victory when it came. Mr Cowling is one historian who attaches much weight to this anxiety (Cowling, 1975, p. 1). Of course, since no General Election then took place, it is impossible to speak about its likely outcome with any certainty. Labour's chances were perhaps better than at any time in the decade, but that is not saying a great deal. The salient fact was that a National government was apparently securely in office throughout the decade. Labour – particularly after 1931 but even after 1935 – could not mount an effective parliamentary opposition. It was an outcome which reversed earlier expectations of inexorable Labour advance in a surprising fashion. As the Liberal Party divided and dwindled yet further, the National government seemed to mobilize the anti-Labour majority in the country. Even if the 'national' idea was in large measure spurious, it had an obvious appeal at a time of domestic and international difficulty. As often happens, however, the size of the Conservative Party and the general security of the government's majority caused problems. Many talented MPs, both the elderly and the youthful, were discontented simply because there were not enough ministerial jobs to go round. A certain factionalism developed, though not one which jeopardized the government's existence. Furthermore, in circumstances where the opposition was never likely to bring about a major shift in government policy, argument about policy took place within the governing party. Foreign policy proved to be one area of disagreement, but it was not the only one.

3

Public Opinion: War and Peace

It is this circumstance that has made it increasingly difficult to identify 'the appeasers' as a distinct and separate group. It is tempting to argue that everybody was in favour of 'appeasement' but that there was no unanimity concerning the identity of the power to be appeased or the precise lengths to which the appeasement should go. In other words to employ a useful distinction, the British position in the world rested upon an acceptance of Britain's authority rather than Britain's power. What characterized the 1930s as opposed to the 1920s was the growing willingness of certain other states to challenge that authority, supposing that the power always necessary to underpin authority was in fact ebbing away. Suddenly, Britain's manifold connexions seemed a source of danger rather than a symbol of greatness.

It was conceivable, just, that the British Empire/Commonwealth, scattered though it was across the globe, might be so mobilized that Britain and the Dominions could stand together against all comers. The resources, certainly, were potentially formidable. There was indeed some exploration of the common requirements of 'Imperial Defence' but it proved difficult to formulate a policy which responded to the needs of Australia, Canada, South Africa and Britain itself. The Dominions naturally looked to their own immediate security, though they still more than half-expected that Britain would come to their assistance in dire emergency. There was no agreement, either, on the likely source of immediate danger. Japan, which had invaded Manchuria in 1931 and had been fighting in China since 1937, looked a threat from the perspective of India and Australasia. But British attitudes towards Japan had vacillated. The alliance with Japan, which lasted for twenty years, was abrogated in 1922 largely because of American pressure. A body of British opinion always regretted this step, and, notwithstanding the Manchurian imbroglio, there was a disposition to seek some kind of arrangement with Japan. Contacts with Tokyo were established through various channels in the mid-1930s but they made little progress, in part because there were differences in the Cabinet as to their desirability. The initiative, however, can properly be described as 'appeasement'. The European situation was deteriorating and it was argued that it would be foolhardy to alienate Japan unnecessarily. The British position in East Asia might be best preserved by seeking compromise rather than confrontation. The 'Japanese question' was but one example of how difficult it was to defend the integrity of the British Empire.

Alternatively, it could be argued that the British Empire/ Commonwealth should be abandoned. The Dominions would fend for themselves better if the fiction of 'Imperial Defence' were abandoned. It was necessary to face starkly the fact that Britain was extremely vulnerable as a result of developments on the European mainland. Britain was fundamentally linked to Europe. Its survival depended upon its European diplomacy. The Empire could sink or swim. No one of importance seriously contemplated this course. More attractive was the possibility that, by arrangement, Britain could contract out altogether from the tiresome problems of the European mainland. A free hand might be extended to whatever German continental ambitions precisely were in exchange for an assurance that Germany had no ambitions beyond Europe. It is not difficult to find expressions of this view, but it ran up against a difficulty. If Germany did achieve the mastery of Europe with British acquiescence, how was Britain then going to ensure that Germany's ambitions did indeed remain restricted to the European continent?

It was possible to hope that the United States would rescue

Britain from the harsh dilemmas that seemed to confront it. After all, in a sense that had happened once already in 1917 and the hollowness of Britain's greatness, in the absence of the United States from a formal role in world politics, was now being exposed. Was it not the time to exploit all the sentimental aspects of the Anglo-American relationship in the expectation that firm American assistance would be forthcoming as regards both Europe and East Asia? The difficulty with this aspiration was that there was little reason to believe that it would happen. If it did happen, there would be a price to pay. It might be a better price than subjugation to Nazi Germany, but it was a price. In any event, it would be folly to suppose that there was real political content in the talk about the 'English-speaking peoples'.

Inescapably, there were choices to be made. Appeasement was a recognition of this reality. Some wanted to appease the Russians, some the Americans, some the Germans, some the Italians and some the Japanese. Very few indeed thought that Britain could survive and preserve its empire on its own. The task of diplomacy was to minimize the effectiveness of potentially hostile coalitions. It also still remained its task to avoid war altogether if possible. Win or lose, the odds were that the days of 'Britain pre-eminent' were numbered. Where, in the end, a stand was made or not made depended upon the meshing together of assessments of economic and military strength, and political calculation. Timing might be all-important. It is necessary, therefore, to look at these vital considerations before turning to 'appeasement in action' and attempting some general conclusions.

At the end of the First World War Britain was arguably the most powerful country in the world. In the victory celebration parade that took place in London in July 1919 units of every race and creed from the worldwide empire marched in symbolic unity. Men in their millions, latterly conscripted, had responded to the call to 'uphold the glorious traditions of the British race'. More than five million served in the British army during the war – its regimental strength at the outset had been only a quarter of a million. Yet the outward manifestations of success only masked, in many cases, profound personal psychological dislocation. The million men who had volunteered from every walk of life by the end of 1914 had little conception of the war that lay before them. All the major European belligerents suffered more casualties relative to total strength than Britain, but even so there had been devastating losses. It was impossible to forget the 20,000 dead on the first day of the Battle of the Somme in July 1916 or the 300,000 casualties over the whole of that campaign. Demobilization had reduced the total strength under arms from 3.8 million in October 1918 to a tenth of that figure in March 1920, but memory could not be demobilized so quickly. By 1929, some 2.4 million people were in receipt of disability awards. The pain could still strike home to families long after the war was over as bodies of men reported missing were identified. The 'business of commemoration' began as communities came to terms with grief and sought appropriate memorials on a scale never previously paralleled in British history. The long process of accommodating loss began. Perhaps three million men carried with them into post-war Britain the horrors of trench warfare.

It is impossible, in a few pages, to recapture the full complexity of the British experience of the war and to describe in detail its enduring significance. One sentiment, however, was expressed in the ritual silences of gloomy November post-war armistices: never again! The only proper tribute to those who had died was to ensure that the Great War had indeed been the 'war to end war'. Poets, preachers, painters all set out in varying ways and with differing degrees of intensity to undermine the traditional values embraced by such terms as 'Honour', 'Patriotism', 'Heroism' or 'Courage'. The 'inhuman' mechanization of warfare had shattered any chivalric virtues that lingered. Preaching in Geneva in 1922, the Archbishop of Canterbury spoke of the 'devil-devised barrier of war': there should be no 'next time'. Some writers, in expressing their sense of 'disenchantment', believed they spoke for millions who no longer believed in the lofty language of governments or the press. Selections of Wilfred Owen's poems appeared immediately after the war carrying the message that the famous dictum of the Latin poet Horace 'Dulce et Decorum est pro patria mori' (It is agreeable and proper to die for the fatherland) should be buried for all time. The painter Paul Nash saw his work as helping to rob war of the last shred of glory or the last shrine of glamour. Such aspirations and intentions could be multiplied in post-war Britain. In this climate, it was difficult to see how any British government could ever prepare to take the country to war again. The view, widely held in 1914, that the war would be a short affair, had been shown to be fatally flawed. It was clearly an illusion to suppose that wars could be precisely and accurately controlled. Once started, they could transcend the original cause of conflict and take on entirely new dimensions: better never to start.

'Pacifism' is a complex concept. It only came into general use as a term at the beginning of the twentieth century. The 'Peace Movement' in pre-1914 Britain included individuals and organizations who approached issues of peace and war from different perspectives and with different strategies. Some took the view that war was never in any circumstances justifiable and were committed personally never to participate in one. Others took a more pragmatic approach. War was certainly never desirable, but there might be certain circumstances in which in self-defence in the face of aggression or support for people suffering oppression, might justify reluctant participation. This basic division, which did not preclude co-operation in peace campaigning when the country was actually at peace, could not be papered over in 1914 itself when men had to make up their minds what to do. Historians have come to use the term 'pacifist' to describe those for whom their opposition to war was an 'act of faith' and the term 'pacificist' with a principled but pragmatic approach. Such categories are helpful, though they inevitably oversimplify.

Given what has just been said about the mood of the post-war decade, there was a sense in which the whole country was 'pacifist' in mood and opinion. A No More War Movement, for example, strongly left-wing in outlook, was seemingly not swimming against the tide but rather with it. Of course, Britain's defences were not completely denuded, but the desire of governments to restrict defence expenditure was not confined to the Labour Party, although this was often for economic rather than for any other reasons. The Locarno agreements of 1925 were taken to be an optimistic sign that the resentments associated with the Treaty of Versailles could be resolved and 'real' peace could ensue. The Kellogg–Briand Pact (1928) was a multilateral treaty, signed with some reservation by the then Conservative government, which committed the signatories to the renunciation of war as an instrument of national policy. There was much talk of the 'outlawry of war'. Arthur Henderson, Labour Foreign Secretary after 1929, described the obligations entered into under the pact as absolute. It followed that force was eliminated as a means of settling international disputes. There appeared to be a substantial consensus in the churches that, as the Lambeth Conference resolved in 1930, war as a method of settling international disputes was incompatible with the teaching of Jesus Christ – a strong reaction had set in against opinions expressed by clerical 'Holy Warriors' in the Great War.

It would be a mistake to suppose that the roots of appeasement are to be found in this pervasive if ill-defined pacifism. Appeasement as a policy did not purport to rest upon the theoretical or theological underpinnings frequently used to support pacifism. When compared with the pamphlets, articles and books of this period in which the word pacifism appears, there is very little material which seeks to expound and defend appeasement. Pacifists were committed to an ideology, whereas appeasers were merely advocating a particular policy or approach in particular circumstances. Pacifists, at least by the late 1930s, did not like the notion that they were *de facto* appeasers, taking the view that their opposition to war stemmed from high-minded principle. Pacifists faced the prospect of possible subjection if their country did not fight with equanimity and courage. They tended to believe that appeasers, on the contrary, were either craven or covert sympathizers with Fascism. Appeasers, in turn, rejected the notion that they were necessarily pacifists of a kind. They might, at this particular juncture, believe that it was in Britain's best interests to go to great lengths, possibly humiliating lengths, to avoid taking part in another major European war. In other circumstances, however, many of those who advocated appeasement in the 1930s believed that war could still be justified. They believed that 'pure' pacifism was apolitical. It had no relevance to the ambivalent choices which politicians were always compelled to make.

It is not too difficult, therefore, in retrospect, to make the appropriate theoretical distinctions between pacifism and appeasement. For contemporaries, however, who could not share our knowledge that there would indeed be a Second World War, the division was by no means clear-cut. After and before Hitler came to power in Germany in 1933, there were prominent pacifists who refused to accept that their stance was irrelevant as policy. Amongst their number, for example, was George Lansbury, Labour veteran, Christian pacifist, and accidental leader of the rump Labour opposition in the House of Commons in 1931. Bevin, the trade union leader, savaged Lansbury at the 1935 Party Conference for hawking his conscience around. Lansbury, he reportedly commented, had been going around for years dressed in saint's clothes waiting for martyrdom. He had merely set fire to the faggots. Lansbury did not abandon his own personal crusade for peace, but the Labour Party as a whole did not share his absolutist convictions. On the other hand, there were appeasers who did not seek to buttress appeasement by abstract doctrine but who, nevertheless, personally loathed the prospect of war. In practice, therefore, there could be an emotional overlap, even if there was not an intellectual one, between these streams of opinion.

It is evident that these confusions were to find expression in a number of celebrated episodes in these years. One month after Hitler came to power in Germany, Oxford undergraduates at the Union passed a motion that the house refused in any circumstances to fight for King and Country. It was a decision which excited considerable public excitement and was sometimes taken to be symptomatic of an attitude which extended beyond the bounds of university opinion. The precise significance of the motion was unclear at the time and has been argued over ever since. On the one hand, it could be taken merely to indicate that 'King and Country' could no longer elicit loyalty. If fighting there was to be it had to embrace ideals which were in theory universal. On the other hand, it was a motion for which absolute pacifists could vote without difficulty – they would not fight for King and Country because they would not fight on behalf of any cause. Expressions of student opinion should not, perhaps, be invariably taken too seriously, but the Oxford Union debate, on an interpretation, was hardly a call to stiffen the sinews and summon up the blood at a time when the advent of Hitler perhaps indicated a new era in the international politics of Europe.

In October 1934, at a by-election in East Fulham, what had previously been a seat held by a government supporter with a large majority was gained by Labour on a very substantial swing. Historians now tend to the view that the outcome was not determined by the deteriorating international situation. At the time, however, leading members of the government interpreted the result as a victory for the 'pacifism' which the Labour candidate espoused. In the same month, Canon Dick Sheppard wrote to the press asking men to send him a postcard indicating that they would pledge themselves to 'renounce' war and never support or sanction another. Two years later, with Lansbury, Bertrand Russell and others he founded the Peace Pledge Union. Not 'peace at any price' but 'love at all costs' was what Sheppard urged on the thousands who came to listen to him before his death in 1937.

In June 1935 the results of a 'Peace Ballot' organized by the League of Nations Union were declared. Some eleven million of those who voted in what can be regarded as the most extensive private referendum in British history wanted Britain to remain a member of the League of Nations. Of these, ten million supported economic and non-military measures against an aggressor nation. Six and three-quarter million were prepared to take military measures. Again, it is not easy to interpret the result. At various times it has been held to indicate both how substantial was the body of opinion which was still willing to support the use of force and how many refused to do so – though the further 'Christian pacifist' option was very small. Of course, the expression of a general opinion may be thought virtually valueless anyway since it is normally only when confronted with a specific choice that opinion forms effectively, one way or the other. There was also the problem that action of any kind was predicated on the effectiveness of the League of Nations – a large presumption.

These well-known episodes have lesser-known equivalents up and down the country. It is clear that there was a 'pacifist mood'. What is more difficult to determine is the relationship between such an expression of 'public opinion' – though it was not the full story – and the policy-making process. Was appeasement made possible or, looked at from another perspective, even inevitable by 'opinion in the country' at least between 1933 and 1937? It is not an easy question to answer. Public opinion is not only difficult to establish, it can also be very volatile. Even during this limited interval specific external developments – Ethiopia, the Rhineland crisis, Spain – caused individuals to change their minds. It is almost invariably the case, too, that politicians, pleading a lack of objective evidence, tend to think that public opinion supports the particular policy which they themselves support. They luxuriate in this frail 'mandate'. Those who thought, as some did, that an attempt to form a close alliance between Britain and France against Germany would drive public opinion more towards Germany, argued it out with those who thought public opinion was longing for such a step.

The British electorate, as we have noted, had expanded considerably since the world of 1914 in which a government had taken the country to war. Unlike the Edwardian era, women voted in the 1930s on the same basis as men. It is sometimes suggested that women were more likely to oppose war than men – though it is a proposition which is impossible to prove for this period. Whatever view is taken on the matter, the relation between 'public opinion' and 'foreign-policy making' was problematic to an extent that it had never been before. How does a government give a 'lead' in foreign policy? To take one specific point: what would have been gained if the Conservatives had gone to the country in the 1935 General Election campaigning strongly for rearmament – and lost to a Labour Party which contemplated no such thing? Was such prudence putting party before country? How much truth should 'the people' be told, supposing that the Cabinet itself knew what was fact and what was fiction in the information it had about German intentions? Was it better to cling to office in the hope that events would cause a change in public opinion? But was that merely an excuse for drift and inaction, a possibly fatal course? Did not government have a duty to 'educate' the people into the reality of events as it perceived them and even resort to 'propaganda' to achieve that objective if need be? But, in a democracy, was it not supposed to be the case that governments carried out the will of the people? It was not their job to carry on regardless.

In any event, governments are themselves coalitions of opinion and beneath the Cabinet stood central departments – the Treasury, the Foreign Office, the War Office – whose leading officials all had views of their own which they rarely hesitated to press upon ministers. Appeasement did not appear on the scene fully formed at a specific moment in time in a moment of revelation. Policy was routinely hammered out and adjusted in the normal interplay of Whitehall between politicians and officials who all claimed in their different ways they were circumscribed by that public opinion beyond which supported their own cases. It was all a matter of politics. Appeasement, in short, was what appeasers said it was and it is to the men who came to be saddled with his label that we now turn.

4

Appeasers

Since it was not possible to become an appeaser by signing a pledge, or by paying a membership subscription to a particular organization, there is no uncontentious way of establishing who was or who was not an appeaser. In 1940 'Cato' published a tract for the times which identified the 'Guilty Men' who, for one disreputable reason or another, became appeasers. The advent of the Second World War meant that those who were thus identified were branded with a mark which many of them would never be able to erase.

It will indeed by necessary to look closely at the leading members of the National governments of the 1930s, but were appeasers only 'born' in that decade? There is no satisfactory answer to this question and the fact that this is the case highlights the extreme slipperiness of the concept of appeasement. There was scarcely any leading politician of the inter-war period in Britain who did not, at one time or other, commit himself to the view that appeasement was necessary as an objective of British foreign policy. In particular was this the case in relation to the quarrelsome atmosphere in Europe in the early 1920s. As Colonial Secretary in 1921, Winston Churchill told delegates at the Imperial Conference of that year that it was his aim 'to get an appeasement of the fearful hatreds and antagonisms which exist in Europe'. Only if that were done could the world settle down. The example of 1914 itself showed only too plainly how ethnic antagonisms and national aspirations could easily escalate in unpredictable ways. His argument suggested that it would be folly to stand aside and simply to wait for an ensuing catastrophe. It was necessary for a statesman to pursue an active policy of appeasement in order to assuage these tensions. On this analysis, Churchill, at this juncture, was an appeaser and appeasement was only a rather novel term for what statesman and diplomats had often attempted in the past as a matter of course.

Labour politicians, emerging into prominence and active government in the first and second Labour governments, also saw themselves as active appeasers. When Ramsay MacDonald formed the first Labour government in 1923 he reserved to himself the Foreign Office precisely to enable him to bring about that mutual understanding between peoples which he saw as a precondition for a lasting peace. He had been bitterly critical of British foreign policy before 1914 and was widely, if a little misleadingly, supposed to be a pacifist during the war itself. Unlike many others in the Labour Party he had little faith in what he regarded as the arid quasi-legal procedures and edicts of the League of Nations. It was necessary to address hearts and minds, in France and in Germany, to prevent the prospect of future war. Britain could form a mediating appeasing role. Arthur Henderson, Foreign Secretary in the second Labour government in 1929, had more faith in the League of Nations, but he too attached great importance to identifying sources of potential conflict and achieving an appeasement. Back in 1919 Lloyd George himself, in a memorandum he drew up at Fontainebleau, stressed the problems that were likely to emerge from the Peace Settlement in which he played so large a part. From a later perspective, he appears as a kind of appeaser, conscious of the imperfections and sources of antagonism inherent in the 'peace' which he signed. Once the immediate post-war emotions had cooled, there was scarcely any major figure in British political life who did not see a need for appeasement in Europe.

So, is the description 'appeaser' so broad as to be vacuous? Speaking much later, during the Korean War in 1950, Winston Churchill drew a distinction which is obvious. Appeasement, he said, was good or bad according to circumstances. It follows, naturally, that appeasers are good or bad according to circumstances. But what are the 'circumstances'? What made the appeasers of the 1920s 'good' and those of the 1930s 'bad'? Churchill had the classic answer: appeasement from weakness and fear was alike futile and fatal, but appeasement from strength was magnanimous and noble, it might be 'the surest and perhaps the only path to world peace'. In the 1920s, then, British politicians and officials still felt themselves, in relation to European developments, to be secure and unchallenged. They could go about the work of appeasement modestly and without fear, seeking to calm the continent without becoming part of it. This was the distant and superior advice of a country which knew that it would not again become involved in a European war, even though, at Locarno, it appeared to agree that it would engage in the impossible task of mutually guaranteeing the frontiers of France and Germany against each other. At some point, therefore, the picture supposedly shifted. Politicians and policy-makers became trapped in a habit of mind which they could not shake off even though that comfortable security which had made it harmless was slipping away.

It is not easy to pinpoint a month or even a year when such a transition can be unambiguously identified. For some historians, appeasement has been seen as acquiring a questionable connotation *before* Hitler came to power in 1933. Disarmament had been high on the British agenda since 'centre opinion' tended to the view that arms-races developed a momentum of their own. The Peace Settlement had supposedly encouraged multilateral disarmament but France, in particular, had not shared this enthusiasm. A good deal of British opinion became unhappy about the 'one-sided' disarmament imposed on Germany. Much time and energy was spent trying to find appropriate formulae. *The Times* urged a 'timely redress of inequality'. Yet there was concern, even amongst such advocates of disarmament as Lord Robert Cecil, that the Germans were drifting back into what he called 'the pre-war conceptions of international relations', back to the belief that they could only rest on a basis of force. Was the continued pursuit of appeasement in the form of disarmament still on the basis of British strength?

After 1933, different questions arise. For some writers, this is the point of transition. Appeasement of Hitler was flawed and futile *unsatisfying, def* (handwritten annotation)

from the very outset. There was no way in which his aspirations could have been accommodated except at the expense of neighbouring states. The only language he could ever have conceivably understood was language delivered from a position of strength. It was absurd to suppose that he was a man with whom any British politician could 'do business' for his goals extended far beyond the particular issues which at first sight might still be resolved by patient and conciliatory diplomacy. On this analysis, anyone who acted and argued to the contrary after 1933 was an appeaser.

By such a definition, however, rather few policy-makers and politicians escape inclusion. To take such a dramatic stance in itself ran contrary to assumptions about the craft of diplomacy. Hitler was undoubtedly odd and extreme, but it was the business of diplomats to handle odd and extreme men, not all of whom were Germans. Besides, it was common knowledge that many hot-headed revolutionaries discarded the rhetoric of their earlier years when they acquired the dignity of office. It would be necessary to allow the passage of time in order to establish whether this would also prove to be the case with Nazism. There was undoubtedly a viciousness about the regime in its domestic policy, but in this facet it was not unique – thoughts strayed to the Soviet Union. Germany might settle down. In the meantime, there was certainly no harm in still seeking the alleviation of present difficulties by negotiation. There could be no harm in exploring what reality there might be in Hitler's approaches. It was widely believed, after 1914, that the naval race between Britain and Germany had been a major cause of the ensuing war. That made it important, as will be referred to in the next chapter, to seek an Anglo-German naval agreement. Prominent appeasers, as we shall see by briefly considering their careers and attitudes, were becoming less sure about British strength, but did not believe that they were acting from weakness and fear.

Lord Reading, the son of a successful Jewish fruit merchant, became Foreign Secretary in 1931 on the formation of the National government but he was succeeded a few months later by Sir John Simon. Simon was not a Jew, though he was sometimes portrayed as one in Nazi propaganda. How Reading would have reacted to an anti-Semitic regime if he had remained in office can only be speculated upon.

Simon remained in office until 1935 and was thus in charge of British policy throughout this crucial early phase after Hitler came to power. He had been identified, therefore, as one of the foremost appeasers, particularly since, as Home Secretary and then Chancellor of the Exchequer, he remained at the heart of government throughout the 1930s. After 1940, he even survived the transition to the Churchill administration, serving as Lord Chancellor until the end of the war. A glance at his career brings out the ambiguities of pacifism and appeasement which have been already alluded to. Of Nonconformist stock, he had a brilliant Oxford career, and rose rapidly in the Liberal era before 1914. In the summer crisis of that year it was thought likely that he would resign rather than support British entry into the war. In the event, he did not, but he did resign in 1916 in protest against the introduction of conscription. The fact that he then joined the Royal Flying Corps, however, confirms that he was not a pacifist. After the war, he seemed somewhat in the wilderness amidst the confusions of the Liberal decline. His talents, however, were used by government in India where he headed the Commission of Enquiry (1927–30) into the working of the act of 1919 which had given a modest degree of Indian involvement in the government of the country. (Incidentally, around this time, Churchill was working himself into a state of great agitation about the government's willingness to extend this participation. It seemed to Churchill to be a criminal expression of weakness: just the worst kind of appeasement.) Thus, although Simon was a considerable European linguist, he came to the Foreign Office as a 'Liberal National' after concentrating his formidable legal mind not on the problems of Europe but on the complex and conflicting needs of the Indian sub-continent. In that role, too, he might also be said to occupy a twilight zone – the *raj* was neither crumbling nor confident.

Sit John was well aware of the challenge which the Hitler regime presented to the assumptions on which British policy towards Germany had latterly come to be based: the notion of 'equality'. German policy was 'definitely disquieting', he agreed, but did that mean that a totally new appraisal had to be made? In the House of Commons in April 1933, Sir Austen Chamberlain, the Conservative former Foreign Secretary, argued that on the evidence so far the new Germany was not a country 'to which Europe can afford to give the equality of which the Prime Minister spoke' (Dutton, p. 169). Later in the year, after Germany left the Disarmament Conference for the second time, Simon wrote to Austen Chamberlain expressing agreement with the view that it was 'a Teutonic failing' to misread generosity and imagine that it betokened weakness 'rather than a warning of strength'. Even so, discussion with Berlin should continue, leading Chamberlain in July 1934 to say of Simon, 'Will he never learn what Germans are?'

The Foreign Secretary's conviction, however, remained that the maintenance of European peace depended upon an understanding between France and Germany. Some international convention on armaments was still desirable and nothing would prevent Britain from doing its best to meet every German claim that was reasonable and just. It was becoming increasingly clear to him that Germany would continue to rearm in defiance of the Versailles provisions. He further believed that once the new regime in Germany settled down and became 'more respectable' many people would agree that Germany had waited fourteen years for 'equality' and could not be expected to wait any longer. However, an arms convention was not forthcoming; whether it would have been of any value if it had been, as Simon supposed, is another matter. He fully shared the widespread conviction that 'We must keep out of trouble in Central Europe at all costs'. It was a remark made on hearing the news of the assassination of the Austrian Chancellor, Dollfuss, on the twentieth anniversary of the assassination of Archduke Franz Ferdinand in 1914. In April 1935 Simon was still striving, as he saw it, to get the balance right: the United Kingdom 'should make preparations as were necessary to defend herself' but should also 'still pursue a policy of settlement in which Germany could take an equal share'.

Such is no more than a glimpse into the mind of an appeaser, but it provides sufficient evidence of his working assumptions. There remained the belief that Germany could still 'settle down'.

It was premature to seek to close ranks against Germany – which could involve British Tories co-operating with Russian Communists – but that might eventually be necessary. Even then, what he called an 'ultimate explosion' might not be prevented. He conceded that if terms with Germany could not be obtained there was no alternative but British rearmament on an increasing scale – a course fraught with political difficulty and financial burden.

The criticism brought against Simon by some contemporaries and by subsequent historians was that he resisted 'stiffening'. He had, it is said, all the virtues and vices of a great lawyer. He could see what cases could be made, could argue persuasively first one way and then the other, but he could not make up his mind on a particular course of action. In 1935, he met Hitler face to face in Berlin and had no doubt that the Fuhrer's ambitions were 'very dangerous to peace in Europe' but there was no direct threat to the West. Hitler wanted good relations with Britain because his ultimate enemy was Soviet Communism.

Sir Samuel Hoare became Foreign Secretary in June 1935 when Baldwin succeeded MacDonald as Prime Minister. He too came into office after a period of immersion in the affairs of the Indian sub-continent, having been Secretary of State for India since 1931. His major responsibility had been to pilot through the Government of India Act to which Churchill had taken such exception. He, above all, was vulnerable to a charge of appeasement in this respect but, like the majority of his colleagues, he found Churchill hopelessly out of touch with Indian realities. His immediate experience did not predispose him to the view that there was nothing to be gained by talking. His spell at the Foreign Office, however, proved to be short. His handling of the Ethiopian crisis – when Mussolini invaded the country in October – provoked, as will be seen in the next chapter, a public outcry and he resigned before Christmas. However, within six months he was back in the Cabinet as First Lord of the Admiralty and subsequently served as Home Secretary – in which capacity he allowed the aged Sigmund Freud to settle and work in England. In both of these capacities, therefore, he remained at the heart of the government. He was in the 'inner circle' of appeasement. Such was the stigma attaching to his career as an appeaser that when Churchill became Prime Minister, Hoare was despatched from the centre of affairs to Madrid as Ambassador.

In so far as academic distinction registers notable intelligence, Hoare was as distinguished at Oxford as Simon. A wealthy and devout Anglo-Catholic (with Quaker ancestors), he had taken a First in History. Moreover, it was not only the past of the continent about which he knew something. In the latter part of the war he had been active in intelligence work in Russia and Italy. In the 1920s it could be fairly said that he had played a notable part both in the expansion of civil aviation and in preserving the Royal Air Force as a separate service. It was apparent to contemporaries that he was a man of conspicuous ability, though his popularity suffered because he showed no disposition to hide this fact. Through to the Munich crisis of September 1938 and beyond, he gave every appearance of being the archetypal appeaser. He continued to take the view that some kind of agreement with Germany was still possible, though he also reaffirmed the 'twin track' approach. He told the House of Commons in October 1938 that the government was not going into the future blindfold. Preparations would continue to be made 'to keep ourselves, and to make ourselves, strong'. The fact that he used both 'keep' and 'make' is an indication – to be explored in a later chapter – of the uncertainty which prevailed on just how strong, relatively, Britain was. Hoare's only divergence from his colleagues in 1939 lay in the interest he showed – perhaps magnified in his own memoirs – in a close relationship with the Soviet Union. He could not be accused of having any personal predilections in favour of the Soviet Union, but he was convinced that Russia constituted 'the greatest deterrent in the East against German aggression'. It was a deterrent that the government as a whole was not willing to bring into play, at least not until it was too late.

It is not customary to consider Hoare's successor, Anthony Eden, as an appeaser. Indeed, when he resigned his office in February 1938, it was widely supposed that this was because he could stomach appeasement no longer. The reasons, however, are more complex. Eden was only thirty-eight when he became Foreign Secretary and this fact was in itself significant. He was of a different generation both from his immediate predecessors at the Foreign Office and from the two Prime Ministers under whom he served. He had gone straight from school to the Western Front where he was awarded the Military Cross for his bravery in rescuing his sergeant. He was only twenty-one when the war ended but was already the youngest brigade major in the British Army. Two of his brothers were killed. It was a record very comparable to other aristocratic families whose losses were disproportionately high. The war left its mark on young Eden and, much later, he wrote about his experiences movingly. It made him an enthusiast for the League of Nations but it did not turn him into an absolute pacifist. Foreign affairs had been his chief interest and he had come into the Cabinet as Minister for League of Nations Affairs in June 1935. His speeches and activity at Geneva gave him a 'progressive' reputation and he appeared still to believe in the League of Nations as an agency for peace. Even so, as Foreign Secretary, he acquiesced in the lifting of the sanctions which were imposed on Italy for invading Ethiopia.

In the Rhineland crisis of March 1936, Eden certainly did not stand out against the prevailing opinion both in the Cabinet and in the country which did not feel that Hitler's remilitarization of the area could be construed as an unprovoked attack by one nation on another. He continued to argue strongly for further negotiations with Hitler. An attempt to restore the *status quo* in the Rhineland by force would not produce a 'satisfactory settlement'. It was quite inappropriate to think of enlisting the Russian 'bear' which only had hatred in his heart for the British Empire. Eden expressed the willingness of the British government to act as 'honest broker' in the matter. It would seem that Eden remained more upset by Italian than by German actions. During his remaining two years in office he showed no enthusiasm for the notion that the British government should be more conciliatory towards Italy as a way of preventing a *rapprochement* between Hitler and Mussolini. Indeed, he resigned, ostensibly at least, because he could not agree to recognize the Italian conquest of Ethiopia. It was the case, however, that Eden had been growing increasingly angry at the extent to which, after May 1937, Neville Chamberlain took a very direct interest in the conduct of foreign policy. It was frustration at this state of affairs which Eden could no longer take. His time would come again.

After his resignation, Eden by no means made life difficult for his former colleagues. He occasionally expressed a mild and judicious dissent but it was certainly not a root-and-branch opposition to all appeasement of the type in which the Prime Minister was still engaged. And there was no one simple anti-appeasement front. It was only on the eve of the war in 1939 that closer ties existed between Churchill, Eden and their respective followers and something approaching an 'anti-appeasement' front was formed. The extent to which he was not an appeaser was magnified, in hindsight, by Eden himself. He may have come to wish that his stance had been more clear-cut than it was, particularly since, as Prime Minister in 1956, he returned so frequently to the Rhineland crisis and equated President Nasser of Egypt with Hitler.

Eden's successor, Lord Halifax, belonged to the generation above him. Eden had gained a First in Oriental Languages, Halifax gained his in History. Both men came from (rather different) landed families in the North of England. Despite a disability, Halifax, already a young Conservative MP, spent three years of the war in Flanders. At its close, he wrote to his father that 'the great thing' would be to humiliate the German powers that be. He was one of the large number of Tory MPs in 1919 who felt obliged to put pressure on Lloyd George to make the peace terms more harsh. Such statements and actions do not suggest an excessive tendency towards appeasement. In the 1920s he rose via colonial affairs and education before becoming Viceroy of India in 1926 (as Lord Irwin) and over the next five years wrestled with the aspirations of Indian nationalists and concluded a celebrated 'pact' with Gandhi which brought to an end the Civil Disobedience campaign. His stance in India brought down upon him the wrath of Churchill, who continued to assert that the British nation had no intention of relinquishing its 'mission' in India. For his part, Halifax supposed Churchill to be rather 'out of heart' with politics altogether and 'rather mad-dogging'.

It was inevitable that analogies between India and the deteriorating situation in Europe should suggest themselves to Halifax – as, to an extent, we have seen also in the minds of Simon and Hoare. In India, in his dealings with political leaders, Halifax had come to believe in the importance of face-to-face contact. Some 'humiliations' had to be endured in the interests of a general settlement. As Lord Privy Seal after 1935, Halifax took an increasing interest in foreign affairs and pondered over his Indian experiences. In reply to a suggestion in July 1936 that there was a certain similarity between characteristics of the chief actors in Germany and India – a strong inferiority complex, an idealism, a belief in a divine mission and a difficulty in dealing with unruly lieutenants – Halifax replied: 'There is much in common between Germany and India, and part of the trouble during recent years has been that the French have been so anxious to maintain things that evoke Germany's inferiority complex' (Roberts, p. 47). The ability of English gentlemen at the Foreign Office to discern an 'inferiority complex' in others was very well developed and long anteceded the actual arrival of Mr Freud in England. Different though they were, both Herr Hitler and Mr Gandhi delivered prophetic messages which somehow had to be dealt with. Halifax, it seems, was very interested 'in getting together with Hitler and squaring him'.

He got his chance, as will be noted, in November 1937. It was hardly the case, however, that the Fuhrer was 'squared' on this occasion. 'We had a different set of values,' Halifax subsequently confided to his diary, 'and were speaking a different language' (ibid., p. 72). But what conclusion was to be drawn? That further conversation was pointless? Not at all. Halifax reported to the Cabinet that, in his view, the Germans had no policy of immediate adventure. Their country was still in a state of revolution. Nevertheless, they would press their claims in Central Europe, though not in a form to give others cause or occasion to interfere. The Prime Minister took the view that an atmosphere had been created in which the 'practical questions' involved in a European settlement could be discussed.

It has long been a commonplace to recognize that the assumptions which Halifax made from his Indian experience proved catastrophic when applied to Germany. Was the mistake not obvious? We have noted that Halifax did not pretend to himself that he was really using the same language as Hitler. That was apparent when the Fuhrer volunteered the suggestion that Gandhi might usefully be shot. Even so, Halifax wanted to go on talking in the belief that, sooner or later, some breakthrough of understanding might occur. The 'state of revolution' would surely eventually cease. Was this now an appeasement from weakness rather than from strength? Certainly, Halifax did pick up many of the contemporary assumptions about Britain's army and navy, which made him cautious, but there was also a pervasive if paradoxical sense that the appeasers were playing a purposeful and still-determining role in the adjustments of world power that seemed to be taking place. The young R. A. Butler, coming as Under-Secretary at the Foreign Office in 1938 after an extensive spell at the same level in the India Office (Butler's father had been Governor of the United Provinces in India when Halifax had been Viceroy), felt that the major problem before him was the same in both cases, 'that of dealing with the "status" of great people, this time Germany – then India' (ibid., p. 48). One could not simply resist change, the trick was to make it as harmless to British interests as possible. The element of almost condescension in this analysis has its physical parallel. Halifax was a very tall man (six feet five inches) and it is to be noted that he refers to Hitler as a 'nasty little man' and Goebbels as a 'little man' (whom he rather liked). Britain looked at these matters from an Olympian height, or, to put it another way, an appeaser, it seems, had to stoop to be conquered.

After Eden's resignation, Halifax became Foreign Secretary. The framework of his ideas had not changed in the interval: 'you have got to live with the devils whether you like them or not' he wrote, reflecting on Eden's 'natural revulsion' for dictators (ibid., p. 85). The best way to cope with them was to keep them guessing about what you might do in Central Europe – a position which also had the advantage of preventing the French from making assumptions about British intentions in this area. It was, however, also the case that the government did not in fact know itself what it would do. In the year after his appointment, confronted by the Austrian and Czechoslovak crises, Halifax came to change his own mind, particularly during the September when he made his opposition known to the terms the Prime Minister brought back from his meeting with Hitler in Godesberg. The 'stiffening' of Halifax cannot be described in detail but there is testimony that by this stage Halifax had come to loathe Nazism and lost all his delusions about Hitler. The pressure Britain had placed on the Czechs was very distasteful. It was a horrid and humiliating business, yet still better than a European war. Munich, Halifax wrote in October 1938 to an old friend, could not be anything but the choice of the lesser of two horrible evils. He argued that with the development of air power Britain had lost the capacity to act as the 'cosmopolitan policeman'. The immeasurable suffering of war had been avoided and the British Empire might yet prove a rallying point of sanity for a mad civilization. So he did not resign. In 1940 it might have been Halifax rather than Churchill who became Prime Minister. He remained Foreign Secretary under Churchill until he was despatched to be British Ambassador in Washington.

Halifax's career, therefore, is a reminder that, when it comes to particulars, the term 'appeaser' is not rigid. Halifax may have 'stiffened' in 1938 and, on some readings, ceased to be an appeaser, but the War Cabinet debates of late May 1940 are a reminder that Halifax still brought what he saw as a rational calculation of Britain's interests at that dire juncture. If Britain's independence was not at stake, he would think it right to accept an offer which would save the country from avoidable disaster. His approach contrasted sharply, though perhaps not fundamentally, with the instinctive tone adopted at this point by Churchill. Halifax, in this sense, remained by cast of mind and temperamental assumption, an appeaser, if a modified one.

It is a Prime Minister, however, rather than any single Foreign Secretary who is conventionally regarded as prince of the appeasers: Neville Chamberlain. It is his name rather than any other which is inseparably attached to the policy of appeasement in its most ardent phase, though, as must be apparent, he did not invent the term. The fact that appeasement is so firmly linked with one individual is a further reminder, already confirmed in considering foreign secretaries, that appeasement was not a simple formula, put into operation without variation by whoever happened to be in office at any given time. Each prominent appeaser had his own agenda and brought to the task of shaping policy individual preconceptions, analogies and experiences. So it was with Neville Chamberlain.

There have been portraits which have painted him in unflattering terms as an ignorant and obstinate provincial who strayed into high politics beyond his depth. Although Chamberlain was to serve loyally under Churchill until his death later in 1940, the hero of the war damned his predecessor in his war memoirs. It is true that Chamberlain did not hide his Birmingham links – but to be born the son of Joseph Chamberlain, a dominating figure in late-Victorian politics, does not suggest a petty origin. It is well known, however, that it was on his other son, Austen, who went on to be Foreign Secretary, that Joseph lavished formal education. Neville did not go to university. Academic writers ever since have had a vested interest in claiming that, had he done so, he might have been more discriminating in his judgement and less sensitive to criticism. The fact is, however, that the clutch of Foreign Secretaries with First Class Honours (those who have just been considered) do not seem notably more discriminating in their assessments or more disposed to accept criticism. Possession of a wide knowledge of modern European history is no doubt an admirable thing but the lack of it does not explain why a man should become an appeaser. In fact, though in an unsystematic way, Neville did read a good deal of history on his own account and possessed other creditable interests. It is not easy to believe that the 'intellectual weaknesses' which, some suppose, account for the failure of British policy towards Hitler, stems substantially from the lack of a degree certificate.

Nor is it a sufficient explanation to stress both that Neville came into national politics rather late and that, as Chancellor of the Exchequer from 1931 to 1937, he had been so preoccupied with domestic economic matters that he was ignorant of world trends and developments. Almost by definition, particularly in the circumstances of the mid-1930s, a Chancellor had to have a broad international perspective and Neville was nothing if not conscientious and thorough in his preparation. The confidence with which he expressed views on international issues of the day may have been exaggerated but it was not without foundation. In the despatch of business, he was brisk and efficient. Even though he was 68 when he became Prime Minister, he was fit and vigorous, though perhaps an old man in a hurry is a dangerous commodity.

In short, few writers now think that Chamberlain became an appeaser because he was stupid or ignorant; he was neither. Where does that leave matters? For some, it suggests that there was also a great deal to be said for appeasement, while for others it remains a disaster but a disaster which stems rather from the vanity, touchiness and obstinacy which they detect in his character (Charmley, p. 212; Parker, pp. 9–11). It is probably desirable that politicians should believe in themselves, but Chamberlain did so to excess. He came to 'own' a policy in an undesirable way. It was these defects which brought 'the tragedy of complete failure in foreign policy and have earned him posthumous derision'. So, when we come subsequently to consider the specific courses of action followed by the British government between 1937 and 1939, the ultimate explanation for its persistence in seeking an accommodation with Hitler, even a humiliating accommodation, must lie with Chamberlain himself. Chamberlain's tragedy, some argue, was that he could not bring himself to accept that he was mistaken and change course. Another individual at the helm in these years, or a more flexible Chamberlain, could only have represented an improvement on the foreign policy that was in fact followed.

It is also conceded, however, that Chamberlain's real sense of horror at the possibility of war did not mean that he pursued 'peace at any price'. He did not leave Britain defenceless. He was not, in his own mind, merely clearing the path towards abject surrender. He believed that he was having some success in promoting necessary 'peaceful change' or at least was only acquiescing in the minimum use of force to allow contentious matters to be resolved in Germany's favour so long as the safety or independence of the United Kingdom was not directly threatened. He stuck obstinately to his objectives, no matter that the occupation of Prague in March 1939 suggested that the premiss on which he had based so much of his thinking now seemed fundamentally flawed.

The power of a Prime Minister is formidable and a great deal does indeed hang, for good or ill, on his leadership. But is it persuasive to pin so much upon one individual appeaser? There were, naturally, serious military and economic issues which had always to be addressed and these underlying structural considerations will be explored in further chapters but, in so far as the final decisions are always political, we need to return to 'public opinion' and the appeasers. A retrospective justification attempted by some appeasers was that the Cabinet did not in fact have much room for manoeuvre. They could only work, in a democracy, within the parameters of what they believed the public would accept. Could Chamberlain have acted differently supposing, for a moment, that he wanted to?

In the nature of things it is not a point which is easy to establish either way. The most recent historian to reflect on this point considers that in 1938 Chamberlain could have secured sufficient support 'either for the policies he pursued or for an anti-German alliance'. It is implied that 'public opinion' was in flux and was simply at the Prime Minister's disposal to channel as he chose. It is not clear that this was the case. As for his policy in September 1938, it is likely that it had majority support – accompanied by some sense of shame. After Munich, the same historian writes, Chamberlain could have 'given up' appeasement and based a policy of resistance to Hitler on a restored national consensus. No doubt he could have attempted such a change of course but, given the degree of emphasis which he himself had placed upon the extent to which it offered the prospect of a lasting peace – a hope shared by many millions as much as by Chamberlain himself – it would have been very difficult if not impossible for him to have publicly indicated his scepticism in what he had achieved without in turn giving Hitler a propaganda coup. It was after March 1939 that a decided public shift was possible, but Chamberlain chose not to make it.

Some historians have emphasized that this picture of the appeasers on the one hand and public opinion on the other is too simple a dichotomy. The making of foreign policy is a complex process involving various other opinion-forming agencies. The Foreign Office has the professional responsibility for both gathering information and offering advice to ministers on policy. There is likely to be some element of tension between officials and politicians concerning their respective roles and functions. In periods of crisis both sides are likely to seek to avoid responsibility for failure. So it was during the 1930s. One early version of the relationship was that the appeasers had all been politicians and their critics had all been sound Foreign Office men whose sound opinions and professional expertise had been ignored. There is an element of truth in this contrast, but it is overstated. Just as individual appeasers differed to some degree amongst themselves, so there was no single Foreign Office line adhered to with unwavering rigidity by the leading officials.

Sir Robert Vansittart was appointed Permanent Under-Secretary in January 1930. A flamboyant and expansive character both in the flesh and on paper, Vansittart repeatedly drew the attention of ministers to the 'old Adam' which he believed to be alive and well in Germany. He was not given to distinguishing between Germans. In his autobiography *The Mist Procession* (1958) he identified a consistent thread in his advice throughout the 1930s. It was also the case, however, at different times, that he advocated an air pact or a colonial arrangement with Hitler. It seems that convictions about the 'black record' of Germany in general did not stand in the way of particular agreements. It was also the case that he had advocated the Hoare–Laval Pact to settle the Ethiopian question – a strategy that could be justified on the grounds that Germany was the main threat but which outraged opinion which was primarily agitated by Italian expansion. Vansittart was by no means popular with colleagues and his appointment as Chief Diplomatic Adviser in 1938 represented a reduction rather than an enhancement of his influence. It would be too simple, however, to say that he was banished upwards because he stood square against appeasement. His successor, Sir Alexander Cadogan, was a man of a very different style. He reserved his personal frustrations at the course of events for his diary and was reluctant to stand square against ministers. There were occasions, however, when Chamberlain did feel that his views and wishes were being circumvented by a Foreign Office which did not share his opinions. He was not the first nor the last

Prime Minister to have this feeling. This led him to seek advice beyond the Foreign Office and to rely even more on his own assessments of political developments. He was willing to be briefed by ambassadors – like Sir Nevile Henderson, the Ambassador in Berlin – whose suggestions and interpretations corresponded with what the Prime Minister wanted to hear. Professor Watt has recently stressed that the Prime Minister saw ambassadors as the instruments of the government as a whole. They were not the servants of the Foreign Secretary and certainly not of the senior advisers in the Foreign Office. He stresses, however, that only in the cases of Sir Eric Phipps and Sir Nevile Henderson can it be said that prominent ambassadors were implicated in what he describes as the 'constitutionally dubious' practices of the Prime Minister (Watt in Dockrill and McKercher, 1996, p. 169). In a circle that became vicious, some Foreign Office officials in these circumstances were not averse to leaking information to politicians whose views were not shared by the Cabinet. Could such 'subversion' of the government be justified?

As always, what was at stake in these manoeuvres was information and the interpretation placed upon it. 'News management' became a particularly contentious area as appeasers felt (like their opponents) that opinion in the press was being slanted against them. This presented them with a justification for seeking to manipulate press opinion in their favour. Some historians have gone so far as to believe that in devious ways Chamberlain exercised 'tight control' over the press during the late 1930s (Cockett, p. 128). He eliminated the Foreign Office News Department as a source of anti-appeasement advice in Whitehall. It was Downing Street that was to be the sole distributor of news from Whitehall. Although it continued to be stated that *The Times* had no official status, its editor, Geoffrey Dawson, was in close contact with the government and is singled out as the most prominent appeaser in the press. It is therefore argued that no alternative to appeasement was ever consistently argued in the British press or relevant facts and figures in its support put before the majority of the British public. Ironically, it is suggested that it was Chamberlain himself who ultimately suffered from his success in lining up newspaper proprietors in his support. He deluded himself into supposing that what could be read in the press was 'real' public opinion. Whether an alternative 'real' public opinion ever existed, however, and whether, if so, we can know what it was, raises vast and possibly unanswerable questions.

To draw attention to these matters is to stress that the argument about appeasement sways first one way and then the other. Appeasement was the outcome of the fears, anxieties and misplaced optimism of appeasers in all walks of contemporary British life: in the press, in education, in the churches, as well as in mainstream politics. Its precise flavour, in any given context, varies with individuals – and the sample we have considered requires a great deal of elaboration before it can have any pretence of being a comprehensive account of the appeasers. They should not, however, be dismissed as a small coterie of individuals living in a world of their own. They responded to the feelings and concerns evident, in varying degrees, in British society at large in this period even if they too readily assumed that their response was the correct one. Even so, while the views of individual appeasers are important, they must also be placed in a more general policy context. The chapters that follow sketch the deeper structural considerations, military and economic, that were believed to be important. Only by bringing the personal and the structural together can we understand appeasement in action.

5

Economic Appeasement

No modern state can wisely contemplate war unless it has the economic resources to sustain it. It is entirely appropriate, therefore, that historians have come to focus on the nature of the British economy in the inter-war period and its implications for foreign policy. Yet it is not easy to isolate economic factors and relate them to the political context that has been discussed. In rightly seeking to balance the emphasis of traditional historiography on politics and diplomacy by writing about 'economic appeasement' there is a danger that every political decision can be thought to have a specific economic cause. It makes more sense to seek to uncover the workings of an underlying attitude of mind both in the political and economic/financial spheres.

At the most general level, it can be said that the structure of the British economy as a whole determined what Britain could or could not do in the world. 'We cannot act alone as the policeman of the world', declared Bonar Law in October 1922; 'the financial and social condition of the country makes that impossible' (Schmidt, 1986, p. 380). The Great War had inevitably had a major impact on the British economy. There was a heavy burden of indebtedness to the United States. Exports had decreased and imports greatly increased. Markets abroad had been lost, perhaps for ever. Investments overseas had been realized for war purposes. When Bonar Law spoke, it was perhaps too early to judge how far this disruption and dislocation would prove permanent. There was still a widespread and understandable desire to return to 'normalcy'. That term could embrace, for example, a belief both in the virtues of laisser-faire and the international financial role of the City of London. It would be possible, after an interval, for Britain to resume its proper place as the hub of the world's commercial and financial exchange. Britain knew no other way to survive and prosper.

Ideas on this matter did not altogether correspond to party divisions. When Baldwin declared in November 1923 that the interests of the British Empire in foreign countries were first of all economic and commercial he was reiterating a Cobdenite orthodoxy. He added that when the British spoke of peace as being their greatest interest, 'we mean British trade and commerce, which are essential to the life of our people, flourish best in conditions of peace'. It was already apparent by this juncture that trade and commerce were not flourishing sufficiently. Unemployment stood at around 1½ million, an 'unacceptable' level, at least compared with pre-war figures. Baldwin, unsuccessfully, sought to persuade the electorate that the answer lay in protection. The coal industry – Britain's largest – was temporarily assisted by the French occupation of the Ruhr but its grave problems would have to be faced at some stage. The 1926 General Strike gave an indication of how difficult it would be to cope with its restructuring – and the same was true of other areas of traditional heavy industry. There was a grave risk of protracted depression which, in turn, might encourage political 'extremism', whether communist or fascist in character. After the 'Great Crash' of October 1929 in the United States, there was even more reason for despondency. It began to look as though the political/industrial structure which had made Britain 'great' had finally outlasted its usefulness. Unemployment began to climb. The Labour government did not know whether to rejoice in these signs of the failure of capitalism or seek to shore up the system. Perhaps the conclusive sign that an era had come to an end was the decision of the National government in 1931 to take Britain off the Gold Standard. Uncharted waters lay ahead. One possible route through them was to emphasize the empire as an economic entity. Imperial preference would replace free trade as the touchstone of British commercial policy. Joseph Chamberlain would be vindicated. The imperial conference held in Ottawa in 1932 went some way in this direction, though it was clearly apparent there that the selfgoverning Dominions were in many cases as keen to 'safeguard' their nascent industries as much against British as against foreign competition. In other words, it might be too late. In the years that followed, the volume of intra-imperial trade did increase and the proportion of British exports going to imperial destinations reached approximately half of the total by 1939. There were undoubtedly benefits from this policy, but there were dangers too. In emphasizing self-sufficiency, the British Empire was following a world-wide tendency at the time for governments to embark on protectionist policies. The danger was that the British action accelerated rather than reversed this trend. But Britain still needed to export to the world beyond the Empire, and that might become increasingly difficult, particularly in Europe. This question brought the German problem into focus.

Since 1919, when Keynes published his *The Economic Consequences of the Peace*, there had been a stream of British opinion which looked to the revival of the German economy for the stimulus that would encourage exports generally and British exports in particular. Here was another area where British self-interest coincided with 'good sense'. The French economy was less export-orientated, which helps to explain why French governments did not welcome Keynes's theories. It was also widely believed by the late 1920s that economic depression would only breed political extremism of one kind or another. Hitler's seizure of power in 1933 seemed to provide confirmation of this theory. It followed, then, that the revival of the German economy would diminish 'extremism' as well as assisting British exports. However, the newly-introduced British tariffs might make a German economic recovery more difficult.

It is at this point that we must think of 'economic appeasement' in more specific terms than we have done hitherto. Even so, we can only simplify a complicated debate among specialists. The concept embraces a wide variety of activities and intentions. There were those in Britain who were prepared: to recognize a German sphere of economic influence in *Mitteleuropa*; to revise the economic policies of 1931–2 where they were disadvantageous to Germany; to make credit available to assist Germany in the purchase of raw materials; and to seek to bring Germany back into a system of multilateral trade. It will be evident that some of these proposals are specific and some very general. Support for them can be located among politicians, bankers, captains of industry and both Treasury and Foreign Office officials. But these ideas do not constitute an all-embracing package. Some wanted one scheme, some another. The reasoning behind them also varied. One emphasis was upon the need to prevent an 'economic Rapallo', that is to say the emergence of a German/Soviet system. Another notion was that such concessions would strengthen German moderates in the Finance Ministry and elsewhere. Further, it was sometimes supposed that informal German control in central Europe might in fact so absorb the energies of Berlin as to preclude more dangerous activities. More generally, there was a feeling that unless the world depression was tackled by some British initiative, European economies would come increasingly under direct state control, whether fascist or communist, and the liberal capitalist order would be at an end. In total this mixed bag of suggestions adds up to a considerable body of thought. What does it signify?

It certainly points to a hope, perhaps a belief, that there could be an economic breakthrough which would avoid war. There was a pervasive 'economism' which believed that states did go to war for economic reasons. Economic appeasement was not an alternative to political appeasement. The logic of the one reinforced the logic of the other. On the other hand, as Professor Schmidt in particular has pointed out, it is very difficult to see precisely how all the conceivable factors – the business cycle, the economic climate, economic doctrines, government/industry relationships, the Bank of England among them – all mesh together to produce a policy which dovetails with the political imperatives of government (Schmidt, 1986, p. 384). There were, too, occasions when political initiatives could be seen as alternatives to any of the economic policy options outlined above. Despite all the discussion of economic appeasement, there remained many officials and businessmen who were sceptical or hostile towards it on a variety of grounds. Some supposed it an over-simplification to believe that the relationship between 'moderation' and 'prosperity' was an automatic one. They were fearful that any steps to encourage the economic revival of Germany and preserve it in 'the economic system of western Europe' would in fact enhance its capacity to dominate western Europe. It has become customary to draw attention to the widespread feelings of guilt among the British intelligentsia for the treatment meted out to Germany in 1919. Even so, there remained the occasional economist who retained deep suspicions of German objectives.

Anxieties on this score spilled over into the major issue of economic debate: the timing, scale and financing of rearmament. Military power in relation to appeasement will be considered in the next chapter; what is relevant here is to assess the economic implications of increased defence expenditure. The interface between economic policy and defence policy is always complicated. It was certainly so in the 1930s. Once again, the positions taken up and the arguments advanced were all, to a great extent, vitiated by uncertainty about the likelihood of war and, as we have seen, the continuing desire to avoid it. Only in 1939, and then reluctantly, was that hope abandoned. Until then, a number of simple propositions could be stated – but they invariably had a sting in the tail. The first was that the security of the state was the top priority of any government. Defence expenditure was an absolute commitment, whatever its consequences elsewhere. In 1932 the government formally abandoned the famous Ten Year Rule of 1919 whereby the armed forces were told to prepare their estimates on the assumption that there would not be a great war involving the British Empire for ten years. There was no immediate consequential action. Allusion has already been made to the political difficulties of increasing defence expenditure in the face of a widespread if ill-defined 'pacifism'. The economic difficulties were no less severe. In a general atmosphere of economic uncertainty, 'confidence' would best be boosted by very modest defence expenditure. Indeed, the figure for 1932 was the lowest of the 'inter-war' period, although of course no one then knew that 1939 would be the year of war. Since the British wished to avoid war, they would obviously not themselves seek to precipitate it. The Treasury, and Neville Chamberlain as Chancellor of the Exchequer, had their sights primarily upon assisting the economic recovery which they considered to be in its early stages. It would jeopardize that revival to shift resources on a massive scale into 'rearmament'. Inflation might quickly appear and a consequent decline in exports would lead swiftly to a severe financial crisis – 'another 1931'. Sir Warren Fisher, the Permanent Secretary to the Treasury, was acutely conscious of the need to be able to deal with 'foreign gangsters' but he also feared an economic 'smash'. That was the dilemma. In these circumstances, it was often thought that the best solution was to keep potential enemies guessing about Britain's intentions – a neat conclusion in so far as a good deal of guessing was going on in Britain itself! The alternative course of seeking to create what would in effect be a war economy in peacetime, regardless of the broader economic and social consequences, would only be justified on the premise that war would indeed be unavoidable. Paradoxes jostled uneasily with each other at this point. A 'steady as she goes' rearmament programme might seem safer, but it might also make it more difficult to accelerate 'when the time comes'. On the other hand, there was always the possibility that it was the German economy which would 'smash'. There were eminent economists at hand to suggest that there was a good chance of this happening. And if war should come, it was likely to be protracted, in which case the careful husbanding of resources would be even more important. There were perfectly plausible reasons for arguing both that Britain could not afford increased defence expenditure in the later 1930s and that she could not afford *not* to increase such spending. And, of course, 'defence expenditure' is only a blanket term. The pattern of its distribution within and among the various armed services also had both economic causes and consequences. Above all, however, it was at this point that there was a need to consider, in military terms, just what kind of war Britain would need to fight.

6

Appeasement and Power

Economic and financial health might be vital for Britain in the long run; but it would be no help if the country were militarily defeated in the short run. The British Empire emerged from the Great War with massive and seasoned armies. The number of men at arms had reached 2,700,000 in France alone at its peak. In theory, a major army could have survived the armistice, and would indeed have constituted a formidable underwriting of British diplomacy. There was little chance, however, that this would happen. The men who had been conscripted wanted speedy demobilization. The military budget was swiftly squeezed. The Dominion forces had no wish to stay in Europe. There were approximately 3½ million troops being paid for by the British government in November 1918: two years later the establishment was roughly one-tenth of that figure.

It would perhaps have been surprising if these developments had not occurred. What is puzzling, as Professor Bond has noted, is that the disbanding of such a major force does not seem to have been accompanied by a thorough appraisal of possible future roles or any attempt to build into the military organization many of the administrative and logistical lessons of the war itself (Bond, 1980, p. 6). No doubt, politicians were preoccupied with immediate problems and the moment did not seem opportune to start talking about strategic deployment. It was in these circumstances in 1919 that the Ten Year Rule, referred to above, was brought into force by a Cabinet committee which included neither the Foreign Secretary nor any representative from the service departments. Even if they had been present, it is difficult to believe that they would have dissented from its underlying assumption. There was no major enemy on the horizon. A few years later the Geddes Committee on National Expenditure recommended further manpower cuts in both the Regular and the Territorial Army and further reductions in the estimates. The axe approximately halved the size of the War Office.

Nevertheless, there was still a role for this reduced force. Its principal purposes, according to the directive to the Service Ministers were to provide garrisons for India, Egypt, the new mandates and all other territories under British control, and to provide the necessary support to the civil power at home. In the circumstances of 1919 this last function was thought not likely to be a negligible one. It was the view of Sir Henry Wilson, Chief of the Imperial General Staff, that the margin of troops on which the Empire was being run was dangerously weak and narrow. There were rumours of sedition and disloyalty in the Indian Army. Withdrawal from Ireland and Iran eased the situation in the short term, but did not alter the fact that the Army seemed to have reverted comprehensively to an imperial mission with garrisons dotted across the globe. It was a case of back to business on the North-West Frontier of India and other outposts.

Yet, although it seemed at times as though that Great War in Europe had never taken place, the possibility that British troops might again fight on the continent did occasionally surface. Under the 1925 Locarno Treaties, Britain appeared to assume precise obligations to guarantee the German–Belgian and German–French frontiers against aggression from either side. A difficulty with this guarantee was that there was, by government instruction, no Expeditionary Force to implement it. The Chiefs of Staff stated that as far as continental commitments were concerned, the services could only 'take note' of them. The Foreign Office took the view that so long as the nations of Europe were convinced of Britain's readiness to fulfil the guarantee it was less likely that the matter would be put to the test. It was not clear, however, by what means the Europeans were to be convinced. The Chiefs of Staff also put on record at this time the ominous statement that the size of Britain's forces was governed by conditions peculiar to each service and not 'by any calculation of the requirements of foreign policy, nor is it possible that they ever should be so calculated' (Bond, 1980, p. 80). Such a doctrine gave no incentive to planners in the War Office to minimize the risks to which Britain was exposed. Europe seemed likely to be able to look after itself and it was wiser, for example, to get back to worrying about how possible Russian designs upon Afghanistan might be effectively countered. The Chiefs of Staff accepted in 1930 that Britain was even less well equipped to intervene on the continent than it had been in 1914 – the Dominions explicitly refused to be associated with the Locarno guarantees – but there seemed no reason to change the perception that the major defence problems were in the Far East and the Middle East.

The statement that the size of Britain's forces was governed by conditions peculiar to each service confirmed that something else had not changed. There was no single Ministry of Defence within which at least an attempt would be made to fuse together the requirements of each of the three services and consider the best overall use of scarce and expensive resources. It therefore remained the case not only that there was no clear correlation between size of force and foreign policy but also that there was no agreed objective common to all the services. When budgets were being cut back, each service department fought primarily to see that the most severe cuts fell elsewhere. The significant advent of air power added a new dimension to traditional rivalry between the Army and the Navy. The RAF had been formally constituted as a separate service in July 1918 but elements in the other services thought this independence ill-advised and sought to sabotage it. The existence, too, of a separate Royal Naval Air Service was also a source of acrimony. It would be wrong to exaggerate the friction but equally misleading to discount it.

Role uncertainty was obviously exacerbated by technical change. The potential of air power was enlarging all the time. The role of the RAF had been invaluable in dealing with internal disturbances in Iraq, for example, but the more general use of bombing posed awkward ethical questions. Sir Hugh Trenchard, Chief of the Air Staff until 1928, put forward the view that it was not necessary for an air force, in order to defeat an enemy nation, to defeat its armed forces first. Air power could attack the centres of production, transportation and communication from which the enemy war effort was maintained. Since the aircraft was a weapon of offence not defence and seemed to offer at least the chance of swiftly terminating a war, bombing supremacy was the target to aim at. There was an exhilarating excitement about aircraft, even about airships, which made the older services seem fuddy-duddy. The difficulty lay in sorting out the truth from the exaggerations sometimes advanced by the proponents of air power. Was it sensible for a country that did not want to go to war to develop the capacity to send in bombers before the other side could? It was axiomatic, as Baldwin was to put it a few years later, that the bomber would always get through.

The implications of air power were also grave for the Royal Navy, which had emerged from the Great War with an ambivalent reputation. It had disappointed the hope of those who had allowed themselves to believe that the German fleet would be swiftly swept from the seas; on the other hand, Britain had not starved. The submarine and the mine showed how vulnerable surface fleets were, at least until sufficiently effective counter-measures could be developed. At the end of the war, with the scuttling of the German fleet at Scapa Flow, the Royal Navy's international position seemed secure – except from the United States. Questions of pride were at stake here. The only sense the British Empire made was as the empire of sea power. It was impossible to see how it could survive if Britain's sea-power was seriously diminished. American admirals, however, now rejected any subordinate role for the US Navy. The British Admiralty resented their ambitions. There were the makings here of a serious quarrel, but in 1922, at a conference in Washington held to discuss the appropriate size for the navies of the world's leading maritime powers, each British government accepted a fixed ratio of capital ships: 525,000 tons each for the United States and Britain, 315,000 tons for Japan, and 175,000 tons each for France and Italy. It was at this time that the Anglo-Japanese alliance was not renewed.

The naval decision was momentous in several respects. Britain was accepting that the size of its navy should be fixed by treaty rather than according to its own inclination. It was also conspicuously bowing to American pressure. One word to describe these steps would be appeasement. Yet the Washington Conference by no means removed Anglo-American naval friction, which rumbled on throughout the 1920s. When he became Chancellor of the Exchequer in 1924, Winston Churchill was zealous in cutting the Navy down to size. The Admiralty was to be told not to contemplate the possibility of naval war against a first-class navy for the next twenty years. And looming overall was the awful possibility that even the most sophisticated ships might not be able to defend themselves adequately as air power developed. A question mark was firmly placed against the traditional bastion of British liberty. It was to be within rather less that twenty years that the possibility of naval war against a first-class navy had to be faced.

After the Manchurian affair of 1931, when Japanese expansion in East Asia had to be considered, it was evident that all British possessions were vulnerable. The decision was taken to resume work on a major base at Singapore, but there was still a reluctance in many quarters to contemplate war against Japan. It would be difficult to win but, even more serious, the attempt to do so might reveal Britain's European vulnerability. We should beware of making too sharp a distinction between the 1920s and the 1930s, but a new situation did seem to be developing at this time with alarming rapidity. The Chiefs of Staff reported to the Cabinet in October 1933 that the defence of the Far Eastern empire remained the greatest and most immediate commitment. However, within three to five years, there might come demands for military intervention in continental Europe occasioned by German rearmament or aggression. It was beginning to look as though it might be necessary to choose between the defence of the United Kingdom and the defence of its Far Eastern empire. A Defence Requirements Committee was set up. It recommended increased defence expenditure, spread across all three services. Perhaps most significantly, it urged the creation of a modest British Expeditionary Force which could fight on the continent. Increased expenditure ran up against the objections that have already been considered. The Cabinet would not hear of an Expeditionary Force because it thought the country would be horrified. Chamberlain contemplated abandoning the Far East altogether. In the end, it was decided to put what major resources could be spared into the Air Force and the Navy, with the Army a poor third. A strategy of deterrence was evolving, in which the existence of a major bomber force would play a major part. The situation was serious, but not so alarming as to lead to the release of all the economic brakes. Indeed, it was thought quite sensible in June 1935 to sign a naval agreement with Berlin which restricted the German fleet to 35 per cent of the Royal Navy's surface fleet and 45 per cent of its submarines. Supposing that this agreement would be honoured, it made it more feasible to think of sending a fleet to Singapore. All the time, it was a matter of balance between the claims of the Far East and those of Europe.

That balance was tilted yet more heavily in an unfavourable direction by the Abyssinian crisis of 1935. Hitherto it had not been thought necessary to consider Italy as a hostile power. That position now changed. The Royal Navy was superior to the Italian navy but Italian air attacks in the Mediterranean could be decidedly uncomfortable. The Mediterranean fleet was withdrawn from Malta to Alexandria as a precaution. The First Lord of the Admiralty pointed out that conflict in the Mediterranean could only encourage the Japanese in East Asia. The Defence Requirements Committee again advocated increased expenditure and talked of being ready for a war in early 1939. But it also drew attention to what it believed to be a massive expansion of the *Luftwaffe*. The Germans might be able to inflict such damage within a matter of weeks that a collapse of civilian morale would occur on a scale which would make it impossible for Britain to continue to resist.

Such observations, and many others like them in the months and years immediately following, all seemed to point to one central conclusion. If Britain were to find itself simultaneously at war with Germany, Italy and Japan it would lose. The military looked to foreign policy to avoid such as contest. Preventing an Italo–German alliance looked the most straightforward option. There had been scepticism, in any event, about the wisdom of talk of sanctions – and the Italian hostility to which they would give rise – merely to uphold the dubious civilization of independent Abyssinia. There was doubt about the exact state of Italo–German relations. In the further complication of the Spanish Civil War, which broke out in July 1936, Italy and Germany might seem rivals for influence as much as fascist partners. There were also increasing difficulties at the other end of the Mediterranean, particularly in Palestine, where keeping the peace sucked in increasing numbers of British troops. Such developments further hindered the creation of a British Expeditionary Force designed for the continent. The new Prime Minister, Neville Chamberlain, put the BEF low among his priorities. Troops might be available for the continent but only if the world situation permitted.

It comes as no surprise, therefore, to find that in late 1937 and early 1938 it looked as though Britain could play no military role in Europe whatsoever. There was nothing which could conceivably have been done to prevent the *Anschluss* of Austria to Germany in March 1938. Czechoslovakia was obviously in some jeopardy but the Chiefs of Staff expressed the opinion that there was nothing that Britain and its potential allies could do by sea, on land, or in the air to prevent the military defeat of Czechoslovakia. The only thing that could be done was to seek to defeat Germany in what would be a prolonged struggle. In all likelihood, both Italy and Japan would exploit that war for their own ends. It would not be a limited European engagement but a world war. The Air Staff subsequently advised against immediate reprisal action at a time when adequate measures of defence were far from complete. The weight of advice being received by the Cabinet was such that it would have been a very brave, not to say foolhardy, Prime Minister who ignored it. It may not explain 'appeasement in action' in 1938–9 but it does explain why no one rushed to war.

Of course, this is only one side of the story. To some extent both military men and politicians reinforced each other's fears and prejudices. The deductions and assumptions made in Britain rested on perceptions of the reality of German military might which may simply have been wrong. What had happened in Germany since 1933 was very difficult to understand and there was a temptation, to which many yielded, to believe that the kind of state that Germany seemed to be becoming could transform itself more speedily and comprehensively into a major military power than the kind of democracy Britain was. Historians have subsequently tended to argue that German power was exaggerated during these years, but it is important to remember that the information which leads many of them to this conclusion was not available at the time. Just what information was available to the British government and how it was gained has understandably become a topic of intense interest. Gaps still exist, and some will probably remain unfilled, but certain broad conclusions have been drawn in which a certain confidence can be placed. Even so, intelligence is a notoriously heady commodity and rarely permits only one interpretation. Analysts, no less than the politicians to whom their information is conveyed, can shape data into patterns that tell them what they want to know. Thus, according to Professor Wark, prior to 1936 the intelligence community underrated the military potential of Germany; between 1936 and 1938 it overreacted to its earlier misjudgement and exaggerated the capacity of the German armed forces; and after the Munich crisis, it came to a more 'balanced' assessment of German strengths and weaknesses which underpinned, if it did not cause, greater confidence on the British side. Arguably, the same data could have been given a more optimistic interpretation even in September 1938 (Wark, 1985, pp. 235–60). As always, there had to be a leap between paper assessments of German strength and a coherent interpretation of its purpose. There has been a tendency, therefore, to argue that in these critical months the British government allowed itself to be frightened by a phantom. Germany, it is said, was not in a condition to fight a lengthy war but, as Professor Murray puts it, Western pusillanimity allowed Hitler to think that he could get away with a limited war against Czechoslovakia. The 'worst-case' scenario which had become dominant was too bleak. Italy was not likely to join in a war. Japan was bogged down in China. The German army had neither the reserve strength nor the economic base to win major victories in either the east or the west. The German navy could not have protected the vital ore supplies from Scandinavia (Murray, 1984, p. 362).

It can be said, however, that there was greater confidence in early 1939. In February the Cabinet was prepared to contemplate a full-scale continental army, whereas a few years earlier it had shelved even the proposed Expeditionary Force. There was a new willingness to enter into staff talks with the French. These fresh signs of energy and determination stemmed perhaps from an increased confidence in Britain's ability to defend itself against air attack, thanks to the increased number of fighter squadrons and the availability of radar. Yet there was still a great deal of apprehension. It was all very well to press the rearmament button firmly, but there would be an economic price to pay. The more gloomy thought that Britain would be bankrupt within two years. The fate of its eastern empire still looked bleak. Japan might not act immediately and might make its own decisions independently of Germany, but act at some point it would. The sad paradox may have been that the conjuncture of factors which produced this restrained and qualified optimism might have acted as an effective deterrent if it had been produced a year earlier. In military terms, Chamberlain might have had some reason to believe that Hitler ought to be deterred from launching a war at all. The tragedy was that it was difficult for Hitler, after the diplomatic/military adventures of 1938–9, not to believe that he could once again raise the stakes and cause the British to back down. It is to these episodes that we must now turn.

7

Appeasement in Action

So far, we have concentrated upon the assumptions, spoken and unspoken, made by those in positions of authority. We now know much more than most of their contemporaries about the advice received by ministers and the calculations that informed their decisions. It is easy to become so absorbed in assessing the complex linkages among the assumptions and values of British political life, technical issues in economics, and complex strategic problems in talking about 'appeasement' as to ignore the public drama. This chapter seeks to redress the balance by looking at what actually happened. The emphasis moves from factors to actors, from the corporate perceptions of 'the Treasury' or 'the Foreign Office' or even of 'Britain' and 'Germany' to particular crises and the responses made to them. How did 'the appeasers' react?

When Hitler came to power at the end of January 1933 there was certainly cause for alarm, but not for panic. He was an extraordinary man who would not make a good member of a London club. But that would be equally true of Mussolini or Stalin. It was the business of diplomacy to deal with extraordinary men. There were obvious questions. Was Hitler sane? Was he a man of the left or the right? Would there be a 'new beginning' in German foreign policy or would there be continuity? Was he a careful planner or did he respond to events intuitively and inspirationally? Was *Mein Kampf* an early folly or a textbook for the future? All these, and other questions were asked at the time. They have been asked, at great length, by historians since. There was variety then and there is variety now in the responses given. That such diversity was and is possible suggests that it would have been very surprising if a British government had decided that no negotiation with him was possible. There were, indeed, early signs that Hitler did not seem particularly hostile to Britain. And perhaps it is true that he had an admiration for the islanders and hoped it would be possible to do business with them. They were in a different category from France or the Soviet Union. It might not be possible to reach an alliance with them, but there was no need to regard them as inveterate enemies unyieldingly opposed to German expansion, particularly in Eastern Europe.

The Disarmament Conference had begun in Geneva in 1932 and it was in this general context that the British government had to make its initial decisions concerning the new German administration. MacDonald, the Prime Minister, in his late sixties and lacking a power base of his own, was fading but always flattered himself on his insight into European politics. Sir John Simon, the Foreign Secretary, had a shrewd legal mind which seemed to be capable of expounding any policy. It happened that in their respective Labour and Liberal pasts they had both been very critical of the decision to go to war in 1914. They belonged to a different generation from the youthful Hitler. On the British side it was the young Anthony Eden, likewise a war veteran, who found himself, as Simon's Parliamentary Under Secretary, leading the British delegation at the Geneva conference. France and Germany were at loggerheads. How far should the British go in trying to prevent a breakdown of the conference – Germany had already left on a previous occasion and been wooed back by Britain – and on what basis?

Mussolini came forward with a four-power pact proposal. The British dilemma was clear. Without an agreement, Germany would withdraw and rearm; but there was, equally, a limit to the pressure which could be put on France. Hitler meanwhile gave various interviews to British journalists and others in which he expressed his hope that 'the two great Germanic nations' could work together. But was not German rearmament already taking place? There were British suspicions that this was so, but little disposition to join

France in a policy of sanctions. Hitler finally decided to pull out in October, despite the fact that the French had shown themselves to be more conciliatory than when the conference opened. Moreover, the relatively mild manner of his departure and his apparent interest in some kind of arrangement made it seem sensible to MacDonald, for another six months, to try to persuade the Germans to return, or at least to open bilateral discussions. There was a disposition to think that some of the men surrounding Hitler were more sinister than Hitler himself. The murders of 30 June 1934 were taken to indicate the insecurity of Hitler's position and his determination to do away with the 'wild men' or the 'murder gang'.

In retrospect, it appears that Hitler was singularly lucky in that the Disarmament Conference was taking place when he came to power. No British government, granted public sentiment, could have been seen to scupper it. Hitler was able to continue the less and less clandestine expansion of the *Wehrmacht* – which had begun, though much more modestly, before he came to power – in this knowledge. One can only speculate as to whether there might have been a different response if there had been no conference. Although Hitler did not formally announce German rearmament until March 1935, it was not a secret. In the first two year of his regime he had achieved by unilateral action what his predecessors had failed to achieve by negotiation. Some Foreign Office officials still advised ministers that Germany might be willing to pay a diplomatic price for the international legalization of this action, but that was optimistic. Hitler, however, could now threaten the use of force as an ingredient in a wider campaign to release Germany from other enduring aspects of the Versailles Treaty. The outlook, according to MacDonald, was deplorable. Prior to Hitler's accession to power the Germans had known that Britain no longer favoured trying to enforce the armaments limitations of Versailles. Their behaviour had revived anxieties about 'German militarism'. A decade earlier, when he was Foreign Secretary in his own government, MacDonald had shown skill in handling Franco-German relations. In the new circumstances, it was perhaps time for Britain to lean rather more in the direction of Paris. Few leading members of the government had close relations with their French counterparts at this time; nevertheless, in the new climate, greater Franco-British intimacy was desirable. However, everything that had happened since 1919 showed how difficult it was to achieve this on a lasting basis. Security remained the major French concern, and British ministers were left in no doubt that Britain too would have to commit itself to some specific steps if France was formally to acquiesce in German rearmament. Simon was prepared to countenance Franco-British staff talks, but the Cabinet was not. What was under discussion was a British scheme to achieve a German return to the League of Nations and an agreed limitation of German armed forces alongside an eastern pact, a Danubian pact and an air pact, all designed to reassure the French. Simon indicated his willingness to go in person to Berlin to negotiate such an arrangement. Ten days before his departure came Hitler's announcement of the reintroduction of conscription and the creation of an army of half a million men. There was a British note of protest, but Simon and Eden went ahead with their visit, though to no immediate result. However, three months later, in mid-June, the Anglo-German naval agreement was signed. We have noted its supposed advantages from the standpoint of the Royal Navy, but its signature displeased the French greatly, both because they were not consulted in advance and because it sanctioned a very much larger German navy than was permitted by the Treaty of Versailles.

Two months earlier, reacting to Hitler's rearmament announcement, MacDonald and Simon had met their French and Italian counterparts at Stresa. A 'front' seemed in process of consolidation, motivated by a common anxiety about German intentions. The subsequent British action seemed hardly helpful to such a development. In fact, there were also even greater impediments. The inclusion of Mussolini, who was worried about Austria and Hungary, meant that the front could hardly be classified as a grouping of democratic states confronting fascism. That substantial section of British opinion which wanted foreign associations to be limited to the ideologically acceptable was not pleased at the company MacDonald was keeping. More generally, there was disquiet about even a loose association which might convey the impression that Germany was about to be 'encircled'. Although the sentiment had begun on the left, it was now fairly generally argued that even the semblance of a return to the alliance divisions of pre-1914 Europe would be likely to increase tension rather than promote stability. French ministers, however, were less apprehensive on this score. Attaching great importance to the Italian connexion, they were willing to accept the possibility of Italian expansion into Ethiopia, provided that certain French interests were safeguarded. Paris could remove troops from the Italian frontier and despatch them to northern France. Italy could move troops from the French frontier and send them into Africa. Mussolini may have thought that the British would be similarly understanding if he offered them something concerning the Italian fleet in the Mediterranean, but that was unlikely.

When the Ethiopian crisis erupted, Britain had a new Prime Minister and a new Foreign Secretary: Stanley Baldwin and Samuel Hoare. MacDonald had always had a keen interest in foreign affairs. Baldwin, despite regular visits to a certain foreign spot, Aix-les-Bains, was not generally believed to share this interest deeply. It would be wrong to think of him as quite indifferent to foreign policy but he was not tempted to intervene in detail if it could be avoided. Hoare had just successfully piloted the massive Government of India Bill through the House of Commons. Given time, he could have been expected to display a comparable mastery over the whole field of foreign affairs. As perhaps always happens at such transitional points, the voices of officials were particularly potent now. Sir Robert Vansittart, the Permanent Under Secretary at the Foreign Office, was not one to be slow to put his new minister in the picture. Sanctions against Italy did not please Vansittart, who had a lively conception of German intentions. He became very active in drawing up schemes to partition Ethiopia. The Italians would get a great deal of territory but not everything. Arguably, Vansittart overstepped the mark in pressing his proposal in the way he did. When the final scheme that was being discussed with Laval leaked out there was a political storm. Hoare had to resign; Vansittart, though politicians who were aware of what was going on were privately equally critical of his role, did not. Instead, he turned his fertile mind to considering a quite different scheme which was floating around in various forms during these years: the return to Germany of its former colonies as a part of a general settlement. In due course, Mussolini was triumphant, acquiring more of Ethiopia than the discredited Hoare-Laval pact would have allocated him. There arose a grave danger that an ideological axis between Berlin and Rome would be formed where none had previously existed.

Although Germany was not directly involved in the Ethiopian crisis, what happened there clearly had an important general bearing on British policy towards Europe. The Italian action had been brought before the League of Nations and the affair had been widely seen as a test-case for that organization's effectiveness. It had failed, but many of the League's supporters in Britain still refused to believe this. They argued that it could still succeed and its failure in this case had been due to the lack of zeal in promoting sanctions, chiefly on the part of Britain and France. Everybody would have to try harder next time to make collective security work. Hoare's successor as Foreign Secretary, Anthony Eden, was still widely identified with the League of Nations, but in official circles scepticism was rampant. Vansittart's activities were not a return to the old diplomacy, for the old diplomacy would have handled it with greater discretion. Mussolini had been neither stopped nor bought off. The entire episode was a comprehensive muddle which had also done nothing to improve the general tone of Franco-British relations. Hitler, for his part, saw an opportunity to take action in Europe and achieve a goal which had eluded earlier German governments.

The demilitarized zones of the Rhineland had been set up under the Versailles Treaty and voluntarily reaffirmed under the Locarno agreement. Britain and Italy undertook to guarantee the arrangement but it was open to question what this actually entailed, and the British had never been too anxious to find out. In the first eighteen months after January 1933, Hitler reaffirmed his acceptance of demilitarization, though he did so with pain. It was distressing that nearly a quarter of the inhabitants of the Reich lived a demilitarized existence – but he seemed prepared to acquiesce in it a little longer. On 13 January 1935 90 per cent of the electorate of the Saar voted to unite with the Reich. Judging this verdict to be a sign that the Rhineland zone might be next on the agenda, the British cabinet on the following day recorded the view that demilitarization was not a vital British interest. To the dismay of the French, the British government clearly regarded any German violation of the relevant articles in a different light from an attack on France or Belgium. It was not evident in these circumstances what the French reaction would be, and the British government did not wish to encourage the notion that it could be relied upon for support. By February 1936, Eden was recommending to a committee of senior Cabinet members that Paris and London should enter into negotiation for the surrender of their rights in the zones 'while such surrender still has got a bargaining value'. Unfortunately for Eden, it was in that very month that Hitler determined upon action which would remove that card from the British Foreign Secretary's hand. There were, of course, risks for him in embarking on a military coup, as some of his generals pointed out, but Hitler's confidence was growing. The operation would be a success so long as it could be kept a surprise. On 7 March that confidence was justified. German troops marched in and subsequently encountered no opposition.

Both Britain and France had been expecting that Hitler would raise the issue of the Rhineland as a topic for negotiation. The British, and Eden in particular, were annoyed not so much by the action in itself as by the fact that Hitler would not now have to make any concession in return. A substantial body of British opinion saw the German action as regrettable in manner but unexceptionable in substance. Another obsolete aspect of the Versailles settlement had been removed. Predictably, opinion in France was less sanguine, but Hitler's timing was masterly. The French government of the time was only a caretaker one. Its parliamentary circumstances made a call to arms unlikely. A visit to London was a better idea. It would help to explain French inaction if it could be made clear that the British would not offer support. Flandin, the Foreign Minister, asked Baldwin and Eden for support in the actions which he claimed France was about to take. It was not forthcoming, though there was an offer of staff talks. Eden thought there was more to be gained by accepting the *fait accompli* and taking seriously the new proposals Hitler had obligingly placed on the table for a full-scale non-aggression pact and air agreement.

The Rhineland affair has been frequently seen as 'the last chance' but, as Mr Bell has stressed, it was not the last chance to stop Hitler without war. France had, indeed, the opportunity to stop Hitler, but only by going to war (Bell, 1986, p. 211). Had France taken this option, it might have been successful, though the encounter would probably have been no pushover. One can only speculate on what would have happened to Hitler personally in that event and how the French would have sustained their position in Germany. The fact remains, however, that there was not the will in France to undertake any such expedition. Equally certainly, there was no desire in Britain to stimulate the French into embarking on such an operation.

Subsequently, the Rhineland crisis has been seen as the first conspicuous failure of appeasement. In one sense, it was, but it has also to be stressed that the contemporary reaction was characterized by annoyance rather than failure. The concept of a demilitarized zone was an anachronism. It perpetuated that German sense of inferiority which precluded a deeper and more lasting settlement. On the other hand, it would probably have to be faced that once the remilitarization of the Rhineland had been completed, the scope of the French army would be that much further reduced. There was also the possibility that Belgium would drift back into neutrality, though the speed with which this in fact occurred came as a surprise in London. Both of these developments forced British ministers to begin to reflect on the significance of France and the Low Countries for the security of Britain. No very positive action resulted. As has already been noted, British ministers thought that the security of the country could be safeguarded by means other than a continental military commitment.

Meanwhile, through the summer of 1936 many memoranda were written trying to draw out the implications of the 'peace plan' which Hitler had offered. The question of colonial concessions surfaced again. Somehow or other, neither side could seem to get substantive discussions off the ground. There is evidence of procrastination in Berlin; but in London, too, there was increasing doubt about the wisdom of the various pacts that were apparently on offer. Perhaps both sides saw merit in delay while they thought they were beginning to put their respective rearmament programmes into gear. As the British Cabinet saw it, little was being lost by the mere passage of time.

In any event, it is important to remember that Cabinets always have other things to think about besides foreign affairs. The issue that was preoccupying the Prime Minister in the autumn of 1936 was the future of King Edward VIII. Once the abdication had been achieved, Baldwin's career was nearly at an end. At the opening of the new parliamentary session in November 1936, he listened to expressions of concern about the country's defences and then stated in the debate that in 1933–4 he had felt that he could not have persuaded a pacific democracy in an election to support rearmament. It was this remark which led Churchill, many years later, to suppose that Baldwin put party before country. Earlier, in the summer, Baldwin was alleged to have told a parliamentary delegation, which included Churchill and Austen Chamberlain, that he was not going to get Britain into a war with anybody for the League of Nations or for anything else. 'If there is any fighting in Europe', he added, 'I should like to see the Bolshies and the Nazis doing it' (Jenkins, 1987, p. 159). It was a wish expressed in other quarters, though it would be a mistake to suppose that it represented a coherent strategy. By the end of 1936, there was a good deal of evidence available suggesting the presence of significant internal repression in Germany. It was still possible to suppose that this was taking place contrary to Hitler's own wishes, but the grounds for doing so were rapidly diminishing. Even so, many British visitors continued to be persuaded that National Socialism had its beneficial aspects. Other British visitors to the Soviet Union found something to encourage them in what they found there. Baldwin's remark however crude, was, as so often, still close to what the ordinary Englishman felt. Certainly, the conclusion of a Franco-Soviet alliance had been criticized rather than praised in London. There was no wish to bring the Soviet Union into the main stream of European diplomacy.

The 'Baldwin era' came to an end in May 1937 when Neville Chamberlain became Prime Minister, a post he held in total for three years. The Cabinet was reshuffled to an extent, but from the existing pack. Eden remained as Foreign Secretary, initially seeming not to be alarmed by Chamberlain's obvious intention to take more active interest in foreign affairs than his predecessor had done. Neville has frequently been described as autocratic, and the extent to which he relied upon an 'inner cabinet' of congenial ministers has been criticized. There is, however, no orthodoxy in these matters and Chamberlain is neither the first nor the last Prime Minister to have been criticized for strength of will and determination. Whether that quality is admired or condemned depends upon the course of events.

How did the new Prime Minister read the European scene? It was certainly dangerous and unstable. A conflict in any part of the continent could easily spread. Despite the different systems of government that now existed, he continued to believe that peace was a common interest of all Europeans and he would work to realize a 'common measure of agreement'. More specifically, he clearly accorded improvement in Anglo–Italian relations a high priority and immediately took a personal initiative through the Italian ambassador in London to seek to bring this about, with recognition of Italian sovereignty over Ethiopia in mind as a possibly necessary concession. Eden was not consulted about this initiative and subsequently neither he nor some of his Foreign Office advisers were happy about it.

Since the partnership between Chamberlain and Eden was to last less than a year it is important to identify at the outset the nature of the relationship between the two men. They belonged to different generations. Eden had come far fast and his time might come in 10 Downing Street but he lacked Chamberlain's all-round experience of government. The relationship between the Prime Minister and the Foreign Secretary is a key element in the functioning of modern British government. An easy-going Prime Minister, preoccupied by domestic questions, may allow a Foreign Secretary considerable scope: but there have been few easy-going Prime Ministers in recent decades. Chamberlain did not hesitate to act independently and establish who was the master. Sooner or later, it was likely that Eden would explode. The problem was not, however, simply a matter of generation or official position; there was a difference as to tactics. Eden quite saw the wisdom of an Anglo-Italian accommodation but thought that the Prime Minister was going about things in the wrong way. Foreign Secretaries, guided by the Foreign Office, often have such feelings about the actions of Prime Ministers.

The Spanish Civil War prevented any easy accommodation with Rome. The struggle itself had provoked a certain amount of passionate enthusiasm in Britain, largely for the Republican cause. The British Cabinet had no enthusiasm for the war. A Non-Intervention Agreement was supposedly in operation, though that did not serve as a major obstacle to German, Italian and Soviet activities. However, at the end of August 1937, a torpedo, believed to have been fired from an Italian submarine, was inaccurately fired at a British destroyer. The British and French governments summoned a conference of interested states and were a little disappointed to find that neither Germany nor Italy was interested. Henceforth, they agreed that British and French warships would attack unidentified submarines in the western Mediterranean. This show of resolution was nullified by the acceptance of the Italian offer to join in the patrolling. Perhaps this judicious mixture of resolution and accommodation would provide the basis for further Anglo-Italian conversations early in the new year. Meanwhile, the Prime Minister deprecated any tendency among his colleagues to lump Germany and Italy together as 'fascist powers': it was Germany that constituted the problem, and by the end of the year Chamberlain had begun to address it directly.

In mid-November, Lord Halifax visited Berlin and Berchtesgaden. Eden was not altogether happy about this visit by a Cabinet colleague with no responsibility for foreign affairs; still, Halifax had been Viceroy of India and, in that capacity, had talked to awkward men. Eden's helpful advice was that Halifax should seek to leave the Germans guessing about British intentions. The conversation ranged widely. Hitler appeared to be very upset that Germany no longer had colonies. As a result, it subsequently appeared in

London that there might be the possibility of reverting to this question once again. It was difficult to tell how serious the interest was, Halifax let it be known that German internal policy was rather distasteful. The two men then got down to specific questions concerning Danzig, Austria and Czechoslovakia. Halifax intimated that the status quo was not sacrosanct but the British government felt strongly that any change should only occur through 'peaceful evolution'. Chamberlain felt sufficiently encouraged by the report to believe that there was scope for discussion. He began to clear the ground with the French. A 'realistic' view of the European future was its management by the four Great Powers – Britain, France, Germany and Italy – and it was up to Britain and Germany to lay the foundations.

There was an inherent tension in Chamberlain's position at this point. Britain had to play a European role but he was still opposed to the idea of a substantial army designed to play a supporting role on the continent. He was not by background or tradition 'European' in feeling, but Britain could not countenance the continent slipping under German domination. It was evident that, in some shape or form, German influence over central Europe was going to be extended. Was that a matter for concern? A dozen years earlier, in negotiating the Locarno Treaty, his half-brother had been adamant that Britain could not guarantee Germany's eastern frontiers (and those of her neighbours) in the same way as it supposedly did its western frontiers. Such a position appeared so self-evident at the time that it had occasioned little controversy. The covert message was that these frontiers could be revised – by agreement. There was nothing that Britain could or should do directly to resolve disputes over boundaries or the problems of national minorities. Unlike France, Britain had declined to enter into specific treaty relations with the Poland and Czechoslovakia that had been created after the First World War. East central Europe had never been a major British concern and it would be unwise to be too closely tied to the fortunes of new states with economic, social and political problems of considerable magnitude. There was a certain amount of encouragement and goodwill towards them, but nothing more. The Covenant of the League of Nations applied – for what it was worth

– but Britain could not become more intimately involved in their security.

One possible source of encouragement in the face of a deteriorating European situation might have been provided by the United States. In October 1937 President Roosevelt made his Chicago 'Quarantine' speech which seemed to indicate that the administration was not totally uninterested in the trend of world affairs. The difficulty, however, was to find out precisely what the speech was meant to imply. The suggestion that aggressors might be 'quarantined' seemed to be meaningless. The neutrality legislation rendered any dramatic intervention impossible – although various spokesmen and emissaries seemed to be sending confusing messages across the Atlantic. Chamberlain was not very impressed. He did not want his own initiatives to be frustrated by American intervention, particularly since he could not believe that this would consist of anything except words. On the other hand, Eden felt that the Americans should be 'educated' in the hope of support in the future. Once again, the difference in substance between the two men has probably been exaggerated, but there was certainly a difference in style. It was the Prime Minister who took the initiative in sending a cold answer in mid-January 1938 to a general letter from Roosevelt suggesting an international conference. Eden took offence, as perhaps the Prime Minister hoped he might. Differences mounted between the two men, particularly on how to handle approaches to Italy. Eventually, in the following month, Eden resigned. He was no longer willing to play the subordinate role in the execution of policy which Chamberlain seems to have supposed he had accepted.

This resignation, however, cannot be interpreted as a dramatic dissociation from appeasement. Eden did not seek to make life difficult for the Prime Minister by maintaining a running criticism of his policy in public. His disagreements can still be described as technical rather than substantial. Eden's disquiet on procedural matters also sprang in part from the increasing strains – which were becoming manifest across the world – concerning the way foreign policy was being conducted. Established channels of official communication were frequently being by-passed in many countries by emissaries who claimed to have, and often did have, special commissions from their political masters. President Roosevelt was a notable exponent of this style of diplomacy. It was also difficult to tell how decisions were being made in Nazi Germany and whether the German Foreign Office really had much say in policy-making. In a sense, Chamberlain was joining in a fashion by using individuals who were not members of the Foreign Office to take soundings and convey messages on his behalf. It was Chamberlain, too, who created a new diplomatic post which effectively removed Sir Robert Vansittart from his erstwhile central role in the Foreign Office. Vansittart's criticisms were often acute, but his manner and pretensions had been found irritating even by politicians who agreed with him. There was some satisfaction among his opponents at the Prime Minister's implicit reassertion of political control over official arrogance.

The desks therefore seemed cleared for action. The self-confidence displayed by the Prime Minister appeared puzzling, even to some of his Cabinet colleagues. The initiative in Europe was held by Germany, perhaps in association with Italy, and by contrast France appeared inert and bewildered. How could a power like Britain, which still lacked an army capable of fighting on the continent, stem the tide? The Prime Minister seems still to have hoped that Hitler's objectives were limited. They might only extend to the incorporation within one German state of all the German speakers of central and eastern Europe. Such a readjustment of frontiers would be disturbing, but it was difficult to resist in principle. National self-determination had become an almost sacred doctrine. It might, therefore, be possible to bring about changes by negotiation and achieve a European settlement underwritten by Britain, France, Germany and Italy. War could be avoided. Events were shortly to put these assumptions to the test.

On 12 March 1938, German troops marched across the Austrian frontier and within days the country's independence was at an end. For weeks prior to this development, Austro-German tension had been high and some such outcome was not altogether unexpected – though it may have been only at the last minute that Hitler judged it safe to annex his homeland. The Prime Minister spoke in the

Commons on 14 March regretting what had happened. Austro-German relations were not a purely private matter affecting Berlin and Vienna alone. He deplored the use of force. What more could be said? Reports suggested that, on the whole, German troops had been well received. Everybody knew that Hitler was an Austrian. It was not possible to come to the aid of a state which did not seem very anxious to survive. Not that Britain would have been in a position to assist if circumstances had been different. The Germans could only have been stopped by force – and Chamberlain did not need to stress in public that Britain had no forces which could actually have stopped the invasion. Only a few days earlier, the Commons had been debating the Army Estimates and there was a general consensus that Britain did not need a large continental army. Some MPs were struck by the fact that Hitler seemed to think he needed one. It had now become clear that he was prepared to use it.

In the wake of the Austrian *Anschluss*, attention now switched to Czechoslovakia. As a result of what had happened, the Czech frontiers had become more vulnerable. However, it was likely that the security of the state would be as much threatened by the disaffection of minorities as by external aggression. The large German minority could be expected to become excited and to press for full autonomy within Czechoslovakia or for outright incorporation in the German Reich. There was some sympathy for Czechoslovakia. It was considered to have preserved a liberal constitution more successfully than other eastern European states had done. On the other hand, there was doubt about the attitude of the Czechs towards the country's substantial ethnic minorities. Was Czechoslovakia really viable? There was a certain irony in the fact that it appeared rather to resemble the Habsburg Empire in its population mix, though Czechoslovakia had supposedly been set up on the basis of national self-determination. Britain had never gone so far as France in cultivating special relations with Czechoslovakia. The consensus of opinion in the Cabinet was that no guarantee should be offered. Chamberlain told the Commons on 24 March that Britain's vital interests were not involved in that area, though he added that it should not be assumed that the absence of legal obligations meant that Britain had no interest in its future. The Covenant of the League of Nations – for what that was worth – still applied.

The fuzziness of the government's position was intentional. The Prime Minister stood mid-way between those who believed that the time was ripe for a firm declaration of British intent to assist Czechoslovakia in the event of aggression and those who believed that it would prove fatal for Britain to become involved in east central Europe, an area where it had no effective leverage. Churchill was talking stridently about the need to develop a grand alliance which he believed would avert the war he felt to be approaching. Chamberlain did not like alliances and thought the notion of a 'grand alliance' a piece of Churchillian rhetoric. There was no real alternative, in his mind, to a further round of diplomatic explorations.

The Czechoslovak government was disappointed by this British position. It was convinced that the complaints of its German minority were being inspired from outside the country. Some ministers felt that the army could give a good account of itself if the German army took the risk and invaded. There was a somewhat obscure crisis in May. The Czechoslovak government alleged that a German invasion was imminent and placed some sections of its army on alert. The British government expressed its concern about the need for peace. The official German view was that no invasion was being planned. It was alleged that the Czechs were deliberately raising the temperature in order to get support from Britain and France. It is difficult to be certain about what was actually going on. There was no outbreak of hostilities and it was sometimes supposed in Britain that the British government's expressed interest was an important factor in the maintenance of peace. Chamberlain does not seem to have been persuaded of that himself, but he was concerned at the evident unrest in the Sudetenland, the area of Czechoslovakia where most Germans lived. He hit upon the idea of offering the services of the veteran Liberal politician Walter Runciman to assist in achieving reconciliation within Czechoslovakia. Runciman would bring to bear a fresh mind, untainted by previous contact with the complex issues of national identity and allegiance. The suggestion was not very welcome in either Paris or Prague, but from the beginning of August the Runciman Mission went ahead. The team interviewed a cross-section of opinion but the prospects for finding an acceptable formula were slim. It was more likely that its endeavours would have to be called off because of the deteriorating political situation in which it found itself. There seemed to be a prospect of some kind of rebellion and German intervention.

The British Cabinet reassembled at the end of August and received reports of German military preparations against Czechoslovakia. It was not only through British official sources that such information was received. Various anti-Nazi Germans conveyed similar warnings. The British Ambassador in Berlin flew back specially to attend the Cabinet. He thought it unlikely that Germany would attack France, but action against Czechoslovakia could not be ruled out. There were differences of emphasis around the table but no conviction that Britain should declare war if Germany did attack Czechoslovakia. It was best to keep Hitler guessing and trust that President Benes would be able to reach an accommodation with his Germans. Churchill talked of concentrating the Royal Navy in the North Sea, but the Cabinet did not believe that such an action had much relevance to the specific local problem of Czechoslovakia. Hitler would be provoked rather than deterred by it.

The Prime Minister, however, was not prepared simply to let events drift. Hitler would be going to Nuremberg in September and much emotion would be generated at the National Socialist Party rally there. There could be a rising inside Czechoslovakia and Hitler would declare that he could not stand aside. Chamberlain had already privately decided that he would make the dramatic gesture of flying to meet Hitler himself. When he told some of his closest colleagues, their reaction was mixed. The political risks in such a step would be enormous. Chamberlain was convinced that he had to accept them. All that mattered was timing. On 13 September, he decided to act and wrote a brief personal note to Hitler soliciting a swift invitation. The Cabinet and the country were startled but not horrified by this step. British Prime Ministers tended to stay at home and they did not fly. That was why Hitler would be impressed. In his first conversation with Hitler at Berchtesgaden, Chamberlain made no serious attempt to keep the Sudetenland inside Czechoslovakia. Stressing his opposition to force, the Prime Minister confined himself to the mechanism of transfer. Hitler agreed not to act precipitately so that Chamberlain could return home and consult his colleagues. The Prime Minister was acclaimed in London and allowed himself to be persuaded that he had prevented an invasion. He was determined to come to an arrangement. In his report to his colleagues, he suggested that he had yielded to the principle of self-determination, but had not gone beyond it. He made the same point in his discussions with the visiting French minister on 18 September. As was by now customary, both countries were testing each other out and seeking to place the responsibility for taking any stand with the other. The Prime Minister was convinced that the cession of German-speaking territory was the only feasible solution but endeavoured to sugar the pill by suggesting that Britain would be willing to guarantee the rump Czechoslovak state that would survive. The only obstacle to an agreement would be if Hitler advocated the claims of the other minorities, for to concede them would make the survival of any kind of Czechoslovakia impossible.

When the Prime Minister met Hitler for the second time at Godesberg on 22 September he was disappointed to find that this was one issue which the German leader stressed. Chamberlain was under the impression that his adroit manoeuvres in London had removed all points of difficulty. Now a solution seemed to be as far away as ever. He was puzzled. Why did Hitler seem so anxious to use force? The German's temper now seemed unyielding and Chamberlain could not understand why he pressed so adamantly for immediate German occupation of the areas concerned. The Prime Minister returned home conscious that he might have difficulties in persuading his colleagues to accept Hitler's intransigent terms. He did so himself, whatever his misgivings, because he adhered to the view that the alternative was general European war.

There was indeed a shift of mood in political London and

perhaps also in the country at large. The novelty of Chamberlain's flights was wearing off and the Prime Minister's stance was beginning to appear obsequious. The Foreign Secretary was wobbling but the authority of the Prime Minister in Cabinet was not in serious jeopardy. A week after their previous visit, the French ministers appeared unwilling to commend the Godesberg terms to the Czechs, though it was not clear that they would take France to war if the Czechs resisted. Anxiety began to mount and it was decided to send Sir Horace Wilson to Hitler with a personal message telling him that the Czechs were unlikely to accept the terms, the French would go to war and Britain would be drawn in. That mission turned out to be useless. Wilson obtained no modification of the Godesberg terms. Chamberlain broadcast to the nation stressing three points: the fate of the British Empire could not be determined simply by the plight of a small nation; his deep personal commitment to peace; and his conviction that any nation which sought to dominate the world by instilling fear of its strength had to be resisted. The difficulty, as he saw it, was how to reconcile these beliefs and he concluded that it was necessary to be very clear that great issues really were at stake before contemplating war. There is abundant testimony to the Prime Minister's depression at this stage of events. He wrote what might have been his last letter to Hitler indicating his readiness still to talk and suggesting that Germany could get all essentials without war. He wrote also to Mussolini urging the merits of further talks.

On 28 September, the day after his broadcast, the Prime Minister was able to tell the Commons at a singularly fortunate point in his speech that a letter had just been received from Hitler inviting him to attend a meeting in Munich. Members showed their relief at the news by cheering the Prime Minister wildly. Chamberlain's confidence revived. He felt he had regained the initiative. The Munich conference was attended by Hitler, Mussolini, Daladier and Chamberlain. It was a symbol of the ability of the four powers to mastermind the future of Europe. There was no place for Czechoslovakia itself at the table, nor for the Soviet Union. Agreement was swiftly reached on the German occupation of the Sudetenland in phases and on an international commission which would supposedly supervise the Czech evacuation. In principle, too, there would be a guarantee of the rump state.

Chamberlain returned to London to a rapturous reception. He had, as he put it, quoting Shakespeare, plucked the flower safety from the nettle danger. Did he believe it? In the euphoria of the moment, there seems little doubt that he did. The strain on him personally had been tremendous and he had shown remarkable resilience for a man of his age. Yet there are also signs, in presentational terms, that he was still looking to the future. He had persuaded Hitler to put his name to a document in which it was agreed that consultation would be the method adopted to deal with any other questions which might arise concerning the two countries. He had risked his entire career to achieve the Munich agreement. He hoped it would endure and inaugurate a lasting peace in Europe; but it would not be prudent to assume that this would be so. Hitler had been given the benefit of the doubt and his word was now on trial.

Hitler himself does not seem to have been unduly perturbed. He had raised the stakes and the British Prime Minister had come flying. The outcome was satisfactory, though it is possible that he might have welcomed the exhilaration of a short successful war.

Munich has always been seen as the apotheosis of appeasement in action. Ultimately, it was Chamberlain's behaviour during these dramatic weeks in September 1938 that was to give the entire strategy of appeasement a bad name. Whatever his initial intentions, it has generally been thought that the Prime Minister's zeal for an agreement was humiliating. He allowed himself to be outplayed by Hitler at almost every point. That has been the predominant verdict of posterity. At the time, whether or not the policy could be justified hinged upon what actually happened next.

Europe showed no signs of settling down in the early months of 1939. Justified or not, rumours of further German action abounded. However, some six months after the Munich conference and a year after the *Anschluss*, it was again Czechoslovakia that held the headlines. German troops entered Prague and established a Protectorate of Bohemia and Moravia, Hungary annexed Sub-Carpathian Ruthenia and Slovakia became nominally independent under German protection. This further step was significant in several respects. Hitler's aims, whatever they precisely were, could no longer be considered to be restricted to the inclusion of all Germans in one German state. Secondly, he could no longer even be considered to be a man of his word. The hopes that Chamberlain had entertained came crashing to the ground. What was the British government to do?

The difficulty in contemplating operating the 'guarantee' was what it always had been. Britain could go to war with Germany but could not defend Czechoslovakia. It was arguable, in any event, that relations between Czechs and Slovaks had reached such a low point that a 'Czechoslovak' state was no longer viable. The guarantee had been seen as an aspect of the four-power cooperation by which Chamberlain had set considerable store. Now one of the putative guarantors had become the aggressor. Czechoslovakia had to be written off. The only consolation was that Chamberlain had been able to show to important non-European opinion that he had gone to the limits of reasonableness and been rebuffed. The detachment displayed by most of the Dominions six months earlier now began to change.

Chamberlain took the opportunity of the Prague debacle to sound more defiant and determined in public. It now seems fairly clear, however, that the Cabinet had become less nervous at the prospect of war, even before March 1939. As has been noted, the military and intelligence appreciations, for what they were worth, were more encouraging. There was more vitality in the Anglo-French relationship than there had been for many months. At the end of 1936 Vansittart had written privately that it was the task of the Foreign Office to hold the ring until 1939. Time was the commodity it could offer to the government. 1939 had now arrived. This confidence should not be overstated but it does help to explain the decision, after Prague, to give a guarantee to the Polish government. It was a remarkable reversal of an attitude to central Europe held by all previous British governments. It gave to a country not on intimate terms with Britain a considerable say in the future of the British Empire. Of course, in one sense, little had changed. There was likely to be very little that Britain could do to preserve the independence of Poland in the event of a German attack. The guarantee was not intended to preclude the possibility of German–Polish negotiation but it was designed to warn Hitler that Britain intended to make a stand. The hope still was that war could be avoided, but this seemed increasingly unlikely. Hitler might still believe that when it came to a crisis Britain would back down.

Developments might be determined by the role the Soviet Union opted to play. One further step Chamberlain had at length authorized after Prague was the opening of negotiations with Moscow. All his instincts had previously recoiled from such a step, both because of a specific dislike of the Soviet state and a belief that 'encirclement' would be counter-productive. The Anglo–Soviet discussions throughout the summer were slow and protracted. There were awkward sticking points, among them the status of the three independent Baltic republics and the dark suspicions in Warsaw concerning Soviet intentions. Possibly a greater sense of urgency might have brought success, but the effort came to a dramatic halt with the news of the Nazi–Soviet Pact in August. An enormous burden was lifted from Hitler. He was free to attack Poland if he so wished. For the same reason, British support for Poland was likely to be of little assistance. The German assault on Poland began at the beginning of September. There was some suspicion that Britain and France might decide after all to refrain from going to war. That proved not to be the case and British hesitations are probably better explained by a desire to concert with France than by any doubt about intervention as such. Chamberlain was forced to declare the war he had always wanted to avoid. Even after its outbreak, there was no enthusiasm for a protracted conflict. There might still be a place for negotiations but, if so, they could now only be in the context of war.

8

Conclusion

Historians and politicians face substantially the same problems. They have to synthesize information from many different sources and reach an overall judgement. The facts may be difficult to substantiate or tantalizingly incomplete. Inevitably, there will be disagreement about the weight to be placed upon various factors. So it is with appeasement. We know a great deal, but we cannot be certain how to evaluate the personal, the political, the economic or the military reasons for its adoption. The Chiefs of Staff advised a certain course of action for reasons that were largely military but from which political considerations were not entirely absent. Conversely, politicians reached political conclusions but they had their own military assumptions. The economic difficulties of Britain in the 1930s do not in themselves explain appeasement but no explanation can ignore those deep-seated problems.

The passage of time seems to have made appeasement less of a special case. The task of seeking to reconcile Britain's imperial role with its European position can be seen to have worried all British Foreign Secretaries and their advisers in the first half of the twentieth century. Some placed the emphasis on one aspect and some on the other, but awkward choices always had to be made. The common understanding was that world circumstances made it impossible to display equal resolution against all comers in every part of the globe. Hitherto, it had been possible to dismiss the difficulties by a display of bravado or arrogant self-confidence. What was perhaps characteristic of the 1930s was that Britain's bluff was being called. It is not surprising, therefore, to find many books which have as their main theme, in widely scattered areas of the world, the decline of British power.

It is right that this global context should be properly understood. Yet there is a danger in assuming, in too simple a fashion, that the pattern of British decline was predetermined. At the heart of the argument about appeasement is a debate about inevitability. We can point to the rise of other centres of power and the extreme difficulty of adequately defending so ramshackle a structure as the British Empire, but does that mean that there was so very little scope for manoeuvre in the 1930s? Was not the anxiety about the survival of the British Empire excessive and did it not, in turn, accelerate decline? There can be no final answer to this question. Certainly, Churchill saw signs of defeatism in government policies and believed that a display of resolution and self-confidence would bring its own reward. It is possible that a greater willingness to threaten intervention might have deterred Hitler – at least in the short term. In the longer term, however, it seems entirely likely that Hitler would have gone to war in circumstances which might have been as favourable as those of 1939. It is difficult to believe that leadership in itself could have created conditions which would be favourable to the survival of the British Empire as it was constituted in the 1930s.

That is not to suggest that Chamberlain's psychological under-standing and tactical methods were flawless. He did not grasp the dynamics of Hitler's regime and did not display a deep understand-ing of the aims, beliefs and practices of National Socialism. He had many admirable qualities but a profound imaginative insight into the mind of Germany during these years was not among them. Such a failure might have been expected in a man of his background, and the misperception was common, but Prime Ministers are expected to be exceptional. Even so, it is difficult to assess what difference Chamberlain's shortcomings in this respect actually made to the conduct of policy. Lloyd George was blessed with much more imagination but his analysis of Hitler's mind and intentions was no better than Chamberlain's. Another set of men in power would no doubt have made some, but probably not a vast, difference to the policies that were followed. Chamberlain, his colleagues and most of British opinion supposed it quite reasonable to believe in a world in which there was an underlying harmony between nations. It was surely inconceivable that governments would set out deliberately to use force. As evidence to the contrary mounted, Chamberlain and many of his countrymen looked around the world and were appalled by the 'horrible barbarities' they observed. Had 'such a spectacle of human madness and folly' ever been seen before? (Holsti, 1991, pp. 234–42).

In so far as there is still something called appeasement that can be linked to the 1930s it can now appear as the policy expression of a deep national uncertainty which was not to be resolved, if resolved it has been, for a further half century. Contemporaries dimly grappled with the nature of Britain as a European power. They could not escape the fact that there was something special about the British past and could not commit themselves to a European destiny. There were other European countries nearer than Czechoslovakia about which even the political elite knew next to nothing. There was a strong disposition to believe that there had always been a British way of warfare which was distinct from that engaged in by other European powers. Such attitudes jostled uneasily with the recognition that a drastic and rapid change in power relations was taking place in western and central Europe. Chamberlain seemed to see himself as both an umpire and a player in the game of European politics and his diplomacy reflects a national uncertainty, expressed in many fields of activity at this time, about the country's ultimate destiny. The policies pursued in various areas – the economy, defence planning, industrial and technological development – may have produced the combination of conditions which enabled Britain to survive in 1940. But those same policies, as Professor Kennedy has pointed out, substantially contributed to the 'loss' of Europe (Kennedy, 1981, p. 293). Does this mean that appeasement was a success or a failure? Of course, it would be consoling to believe that there could have been a policy in which there was no distinction between British interests and those of non-Nazi Europe as a whole. The inability of British and French governments ever to co-operate effectively is a sufficient commentary on this aspiration.

Internal politics always involves the calculation of advantage. The standard complaint against the practitioners of appeasement is that concessions were made from a position of weakness, or perceived weakness, which should only have been contemplated from a position of strength. The general principle may be admitted, but it is not without difficulties. A substantial section of British opinion had no wish to accept the priorities which would have been required to achieve the necessary image of strength. The problem of how a peaceloving democracy can be persuaded to prepare for war is an enduring one to which there is no easy answer. We are touching here on vexed issues of ethics and politics. British policy at Munich, for example, was sometimes condemned for its apparent display of weakness by those who liked to regard themselves as exponents of power politics and a show of force. It was equally condemned, however, by many who had been adamantly against any vigorous policy of British rearmament. It was possible for many people simultaneously to suffer anguish at the prospect of another major war and to feel intense remorse at what they believed to be Britain's callous indifference to the plight of Czechoslovakia. It is precisely because such emotional difficulties cluster round appeasement that this period of British foreign policy continues to attract attention. It is also perpetually intriguing because we can never be certain what the consequences of alternative policies might have been. Between 1939 and 1941 world politics evolved in a way that few observers could have predicted with confidence even in 1938.

References

Bell, P. M. H. 1986: *The Origins of the Second World War in Europe*. Longman.

Bond, B. 1980: *British Military Policy between the Two World Wars*. Clarendon.

Callahan, R. 1984: *Churchill: Retreat from Empire*. Costello.

Ceadel, M. 1980: *Pacifism in Britain, 1914–1945: the Defining of a Faith*. Clarendon.

Charmley, J. 1989: *Chamberlain and the Lost Peace*. John Curtis/Hodder & Stoughton.

Charmley, J. 1993: *Churchill: The End of Glory*. Hodder & Stoughton.

Cowling, M. 1975: *The Impact of Hitler: British Politics and British Policy 1933–1940*. Cambridge University Press.

Dockrill, M. and McKercher, B. eds, 1996: *Diplomacy and World Power: Studies in British Foreign Policy, 1890–1950*. Cambridge.

Gilbert, M. 1966: *The Roots of Appeasement*. Weidenfeld & Nicolson.

Gilbert, M. and Gott, R. 1963: *The Appeasers*. Weidenfeld & Nicolson.

Holsti, K. J. 1991: *Peace and War: Armed Conflicts and International Order, 1648–1989*. Cambridge.

Jenkins, R. 1987: *Baldwin*. Collins.

Kennedy, P. 1981: *The Realities behind Diplomacy: Background Influences on British External Policy, 1865–1980*. Allen & Unwin.

Parker, R. A. C. 1993: *Chamberlain and Appeasement: British Policy and the Coming of the Second World War*. Macmillan.

Robbins, K. G. 1968: *Munich 1938*. Cassell.

Roberts, A. 1991: *'The Holy Fox': A Biography of Lord Halifax*.

Weidenfeld & Nicolson.

Schmidt, G. 1986: *The Politics and Economics of Appeasement: British Foreign Policy in the 1930s*. Berg.

Taylor, A. J. P. 1961: *The Origins of the Second World War*. Hamish Hamilton.

Wark, W. K. 1985: *The Ultimate Enemy: British Intelligence and Nazi Germany, 1933–1939*. Tauris.

Watt, D. C. 1985: *Succeeding John Bull: America in Britain's Place, 1900–1975*. Cambridge.

Guide to Further Reading

The literature that has been summarized and discussed in this study is enormous. The following is intended only as a guide to some of the most important works, most of which have substantial bibliographies. The emphasis in selection has therefore generally been upon the most recent works. No attempt has been made to list the many articles which debate many important details. The most comprehensive single bibliography is S. Astor, ed., *British Foreign Policy, 1918–1945: a Guide to Research and Research Materials*, Costello, 1984. It should be noted that a slip has occurred on the title page and the bibliographer's name is in fact Aster. The books that follow relate primarily to the chapter divisions of this study but many of them also range over other relevant issues.

Historiography

E. H. Carr, *The Twenty Years' Crisis, 1919–39*, Macmillan, 1939; M. Dockrill and B. McKercher, eds, *Diplomacy and World Power: Studies in British Foreign Policy, 1890–1950*, Cambridge, University Press, 1996; M. Gilbert and R. Gott, *The Appeasers*, Weidenfeld and Nicolson, 1963; M. Gilbert, *The Roots of Appeasement*, Weidenfeld and Nicolson, 1966; K. J. Holsti, *Peace and War: Armed Conflicts and International Order, 1648–1989*, Cambridge University Press, 1991; A. J. P. Taylor, *The Origins of the Second World War*, Hamish Hamilton, 1961; a most useful appraisal is G. Martel, ed., *The Origins of the Second World War Reconsidered: the A. J. P. Taylor Debate after Twenty-five Years*, Allen and Unwin, 1986; there are also useful general essays in D. Dilks, ed., *Retreat from Power:*

Studies in Britain's Foreign Policy of the Twentieth Century: Volume One, 1906–1939, Macmillan, 1981, a stimulating overview is B. Porter, *Britain, Europe and the World, 1850–1986*, second edition, Allen and Unwin, 1987; a useful collection of documents has been compiled by A. Adamthwaite, *The Lost Peace: International Relations in Europe, 1918–1939*, Arnold, 1980; W. R. Rock, *British Appeasement in the 1930s*, Arnold, 1977; P. M. H. Bell, *The Origins of the Second World War in Europe*, Longman. 1986: K. Middlemas, *Diplomacy of Illusion: the British Government and Germany, 1937–39*, Weidenfeld and Nicolson, 1972; P. Kennedy, *The Realities behind Diplomacy: Background Influences on British External Policy, 1865–1980*, Allen and Unwin, 1981.

Policy and Party

The general political contcxt can be considered in A. J. Crozier, *Appeasement and Germany's Last Bid for Colonies*, Macmillan, 1988; C. L. Mowat, *Britain between the Wars*, Methuen, 1955; A. Marwick, *Britain in the Century of Total War, 1900–1967*, Bodley Head, 1968; R. J. Overy and A. Wheatcroft, *Road to War*, Macmillan, 1989; M. Pugh, *The Making of Modern British Politics, 1867–1939*, Blackwell, 1982; K. G. Robbins, *The Eclipse of a Great Power: Modern Britain, 1870–1992*, Longman, 1994; M. Cowling, *The Impact of Hitler: British Politics and British Policy, 1933–1940*, Cambridge University Press, 1975. Useful on various facets of thc 'peace movement' are K. G. Robbins, *The Abolition of War: the 'Peace Movement' in Britain, 1914–1919*, University of Wales Press, 1976; M. Swartz, *The Union of Democratic Control in British Politics during the First World War*, Oxford University Press, 1971; D. S. Birn, *The League of Nations Union*, Oxford University Press, 1981; M. Ceadel, *Pacifism in Britain 1914–1945: the Defining of a Faith*, Clarendon Press, 1980; J. F. Naylor, *Labour's International Policy: the Labour Party in the 1930s*, Weidenfeld and Nicolson, 1969. The three 'zones' can be considered in the following works: *Europe* – A. Lentin, *Guilt at Versailles: Lloyd George and the pre-history of Appeasement*, Leicester University Press, 1984; A. Orde, *Great Britain and International Security, 1920–1926*, Royal Historical Society, 1978; D. Dutton, *Austen Chamberlain: Gentleman in Politics*, Ross Anderson, 1985; *Empire* – M. Beloff, *Imperial Sunset: Volume One, Britain's Liberal Empire, 1897–1921*, Methuen, 1969; J. Gallagher, *The Decline, Revival and Fall of the British Empire*, Cambridge University Press, 1982; R. Ovendale, *'Appeasement' and the English-Speaking World*, University of Wales Press, 1975; on East Asia in particular, see P. Lowe,

Britain in the Far East: a Survey from 1819 to the Present, Longman, 1981; B. A. Lee, *Britain and the Sino-Japanese War, 1937–1939*, Oxford University Press, 1973; P. Lowe, *Great Britain and the Origins of the Pacific War: a Study of British Policy in East Asia, 1937–1941*, Oxford University Press, 1977; W. R. Louis, *British Strategy in the Far East 1919–1939*, Clarendon Press, 1971; N. R. Clifford, *Retreat from China: British Policy in the Far East, 1937–1941*, Longman, 1967; I. H. Nish, ed, *Anglo-Japanese Alienation, 1919–1952*, Cambridge University Press, 1982.
United States – D. C. Watt, *Succeeding John Bull: America in Britain's Place, 1900–1975*, Cambridge University Press, 1985; C. A. Macdonald, *The United States, Britain and Appeasement*, Macmillan, 1981; J. R. Leutze, *Bargaining for Supremacy: Anglo-American Naval Relations, 1937–1941*, University of North Carolina Press, 1977; D. Reynolds, *The Creation of the Anglo-American Alliance, 1937–1941: a Study in Competitive Co-operation*, Europa, 1981.

Public Opinion: War and Peace

J. Winter, *Sites of Memory, Sites of Mourning: The Great War in European Cultural History*, Cambridge University Press, 1995; A. Gregory, *The Silence of Memory: Armistice Day, 1919–1946*, Berg, 1994.

Appeasers

D. Dutton, *Simon: A Political Biography of Sir John Simon*, Aurum, 1992; R. Crockett, *Twilight of Truth: Chamberlain, Appeasement and the Manipulation of the Press*, Weidenfeld & Nicolson, 1989; J. Charmley, *Chamberlain and the Lost Peace*, Hodder & Stoughton, 1989; R. A. C. Parker, *Chamberlain and Appeasement*, Macmillan, 1993; A. Roberts, *'The Holy Fox': A Biography of Lord Halifax*, Weidenfeld & Nicolson, 1991.

Economic Appeasement

G. Schmidt, *The Politics and Economics of Appeasement: British Foreign Policy in the 1930s*, Berg, 1986; B.-J. Wendt's essay '"Economic Appeasement" – a crisis strategy' in W. J. Mommsen and L. Kettenacker, eds, *The Fascist Challenge and the Policy of Appeasement*, Allen and Unwin, 1983; G. C. Peden, *British Rearmament and the Treasury, 1932–1939*, Scottish Academic Press, 1979.

Appeasement and Power

A. Clayton, *The British Empire as a Superpower, 1919–1939*, Macmillan, 1986; R. P. Shay, *British Rearmament in the Thirties: Politics and Profits*, Princeton University Press, 1977; B. Bond, *British Military Policy between the Two World Wars*, Clarendon Press, 1980; D. C. Watt, *Too Serious a Business: European Armed Forces and the approach to the second World War*, Temple Smith, 1975; M. Howard, *The Continental Commitment: the Dilemma of British Defence Policy in the Era of the Two World Wars*, Temple Smith, 1972; H. M. Hyde, *British Air Policy between the Wars, 1918–1939*, Heinemann, 1976; D. Reynolds, *Britannia Overruled: British Policy and World Power in the 20th Century*, Longman, 1991; S. Roskill, *Naval Policy between the Wars*, two volumes, Collins, 1968 and 1976; W. K. Wark, *The Ultimate Enemy: British Intelligence and Nazi Germany, 1933–1939*, Tauris, 1985; C. Andrew and D. Dilks, eds, *The Missing Dimension: Governments and Intelligence Communities in the Twentieth Century*, Macmillan, 1984; U. Bialer, *The Shadow of the Bomber: Fear of Air Attack and British Politics, 1932–1939*, Royal Historical Society, 1980; P. Kennedy, *The Rise and Fall of the Great Powers*, Unwin Hyman, 1988; C. Barnett, *The Collapse of British Power*, Eyre Methuen, 1972.

Appeasement in Action

E. W. Bennett, *German Rearmament and the West, 1932–1933*, Princeton University Press, 1979; N. Rostow, *Anglo-French Relations, 1934–36*, Macmillan, 1984; F. M. Hardie, *The Abyssinian Crisis*, Cass, 1974; D. P. Waley, *British Public Opinion and the Abyssinian War, 1935–1936*, Temple Smith, 1976; J. Edward, *The British Government and the Spanish Civil War, 1936–1939*, Macmillan, 1979; J. T. Emmerson, *The Rhineland Crisis 7 March 1936*, Temple Smith, 1977; R. Douglas, *In the Year of Munich*, Macmillan, 1977; K. G. Robbins, *Munich 1938*, Cassell, 1968; T. Taylor, *Munich: the Price of Peace*, Hodder and Stoughton, 1979; W. Murray, *The Change in the European Balance of Power, 1938–1939*, Princeton University Press, 1984; R. Douglas, ed., *1939: a Retrospect Forty Years After*, Macmillan, 1983; D. C. Watt, *How War Came: The Immediate Origins of the Second World War, 1938–1939*, Heinemann, 1989; S. Aster, *The Making of the Second World War*, Deutsch, 1973.

Useful biographical or semi-biographical studies include L. W. Fuscher, *Neville Chamberlain and Appeasement: a Study in the Politics of History*,

Norton, 1982; Earl of Birkenhead, *Halifax: the Life of Lord Halifax*, Hamish Hamilton, 1965; D. Carlton, *Anthony Eden: a Biography*, Allen Lane, 1981; D. Marquand, *Ramsay MacDonald*, Cape, 1977; J. A. Cross, *Sir Samuel Hoare: a Political Biography*, Cape, 1977; M. Gilbert, *Winston S. Churchill*, Volume V, Heinemann, 1976; R. Callahan, *Churchill: Retreat from Empire*, Costello, 1984; R. Jenkins, *Baldwin*, Collins, 1987; D. Dilks, ed., *The Diaries of Sir Alexander Cadogan, 1938–1945*, Cassell, 1971.

Index